Spanish Literature

A Brief Survey

by

Nicholson B. Adams and John E. Keller

About the Book:

1. Literature in Spain from Roman times until now.
2. Short chronological treatment of the principal movements and authors.
3. Tables before each chapter outlining the material, with dates.
4. The last chapter brings the account up to the date of publication.
5. A glossary-index facilitates ready definition and reference.

About the Authors:

Drs. Adams and Keller are Professors of Spanish at the University of North Carolina, the first since 1924 and the second since 1950. Both have published numerous books and articles in the field of Spanish literature.

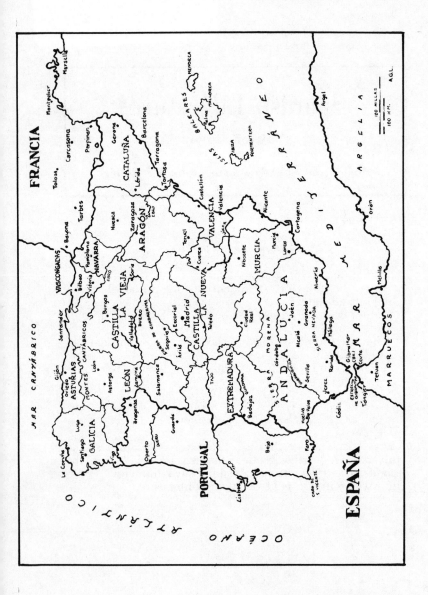

SPANISH
LITERATURE
A Brief Survey

By
Nicholson B. Adams
and
John E. Keller

Professors of Spanish
University of North Carolina

1968

LITTLEFIELD, ADAMS & CO.
Totowa, New Jersey

Copyright © 1962

by Littlefield, Adams & Co.

First Edition 1960
Reprinted 1962
Reprinted 1965
Reprinted 1968
Library of Congress Catalog Card Number 60-3392

Printed in the United States of America

Foreword

Spain is a fascinating country, and has produced brilliant and highly original art, including the literary. Spanish literature is becoming rapidly better known, and deserves to be even more so. If this brief and modest volume helps to introduce Spain's remarkable literary productions to still more readers, the authors will be most happy to think that they have performed a meritorious service.

We wish to thank numerous friends, colleagues, and close relatives for the aid which they have steadily and generously offered.

Nicholson B. Adams
John E. Keller

Chapel Hill, North Carolina,

Contents

Roman, Visigothic, and Moorish Spain.
The Spanish Language

ROMAN SPAIN (206 B.C.–409 A.D.)	VISIGOTHIC SPAIN (409–711)	MOORISH SPAIN (711–1492)
Annaeus Seneca, the Elder (54 B.C.–39 A.D.)	St. Isidore of Seville (ca. 570–636)	*Arabic Writers*
Lucius Annaeus Seneca (4 B.C.–65 A.D.)	Paulus Orosius (fifth century)	Mocádem of Cordova (alive in 900)
Marcus Annaeus Lucanus (39–65 A.D.)		Ibn Hazm (994–1063)
Marcus Fabius Quintilianus (ca. 35–ca. 96 A.D.)		Ibn Zaydun (1003–1070)
Marcus Valerius Martialis (ca. 38–ca. 104 A.D.)		Ibn Guzman (d. 1160)
Lucius J. Moderatus Columella (1st century A.D.)		Avempace (late 11th century)
Aurelius Clemens Prudentius (348–after 405 A.D.)		Averroes (1126–1198)
		Jewish Writers
		Maimonides of Cordova (1135–1204)

Roman, Visigothic, and Moorish Spain. The Spanish Language

ROMAN SPAIN

The Romans were the first ancient people to alter completely the Iberian Peninsula and its way of life, and to give it a civilization about which we know a great deal. Before the Romans came, Iberian, Celtic, and certain other peoples lived in what is now Spain and Portugal. Greeks and Phoenicians founded cities and trading posts there. The Carthaginians, a Phoenician people themselves, were defeated by the Romans in the third century B.C., and by the end of the first century Roman power was supreme in the entire area. The victory had not been easy to obtain, and one city in particular, Numantia, held out for long against the legions commanded by Scipio Aemilianus. The fall of Numancia, as Spaniards call the city, has always been a favorite theme of Spaniards, and the heroic defense of the city by its dauntless inhabitants was treated by Cervantes in a play.

Rome pensioned some of her soldiers in Spain, founding for them cities, for example, Italica. Other cities were Caesaraugusta (later Saragossa), Emerita (Mérida), and Gades (Cádiz) famous for dancing girls, founded long before by the Phoenicians and called Gadir (modern Cádiz), which was a thriving city in Roman times. Roman law, agriculture, sciences, architecture—in short, a whole Roman way of life and culture came to Spain. Roman emperors had their origin there (Hadrian, Trajan, and Marcus Aurelius), and great Roman writers came from such cities as Cordova and from what is now Aragon. Spain was the most Romanized of all Roman provinces.

1

Spaniards like to think that such native-born Spanish Romans as the Senecas, Martial, Quintilian, Columella, and Lucan were true Spaniards. The point could be argued pro and con, for these gentlemen lived most of their lives in Rome and their writing was in the best traditions of Roman writing. During Rome's Silver Age (the first century A.D.) these Spanish Romans flourished and their works earned them fame in the Eternal City. It is not strange that Spain likes to claim them as her first literati.

Both the Senecas were Cordovans. **Marcus Annaeus Seneca,** called "the Elder," (54 B.C.-39 A.D.) was a teacher of rhetoric and a politician. His fame as a writer rests upon his *Controversiae,* treatises on legal procedure. His son, **Lucius Annaeus Seneca,** "the Younger," (4 B.C.-65 A.D.) was more famous. He was a follower of the Stoic philosophers, but in his rhetoric he was highly ornate, especially in his plays. His greatest fame lies in his philosophical works, and these had a great deal of influence in his own and in later times. His *De Ira (On Anger)* is to some his most lasting essay. His ten tragedies were widely admired in the Middle Ages and the Renaissance. He was Nero's tutor and he took his own life at this emperor's order.

Lucan, known in Latin as **Marcus Annaeus Lucanus** (39-65 A.D.) was also a Cordovan and a kinsman of the Senecas. He left Spain as a child and spent his life in Rome. His one surviving work, upon which his fame rests, was his *Pharsalia,* also known as *De Bello Civili.* It is an epic poem in ten books about the wars between Caesar and Pompey. His showy rhetoric was famous, and because of Seneca the Younger, Lucan, and two other Cordovans, Juan de Mena and Góngora, some have thought that there must be something in the air of Cordova which produces ornateness.

Marcus Valerius Martialis (ca. 38-ca. 104 A.D.), known as Martial, was a native of Bilbilis, now Calatayud, Aragon. He lived in Rome and knew the great writers of the times. His *Epigrams,* which appeared in a number of volumes, were elegiac poems for the most part, but he varied his meters and in this respect differed from the models set up by the Greeks. The subjects of the *Epigrams* cover all the phases of life among Rome's young sophisticates in the first century, not omitting the scabrous.

Marcus Fabius Quintilianus, known to us as Quintilian

(ca. 35-ca. 96 A.D.), was from Calahorra. His greatest work was *Institutio Oratoria*, a kind of manual on the training of public speakers. In his youth he felt the influence of Seneca the Younger, but in his mature years his greatest model was Cicero.

Lucius Junius Moderatus Columella of the first century A.D. held large estates near his native Gades (Cádiz) and in Italy. His twelve books, *De Re Rustica,* treat agriculture in great detail and show him as the ancestor of modern scientific farmers. He is regarded as the foremost agronomist of antiquity.

Aurelius Clemens Prudentius, born probably at Saragossa in 348 A.D., spent most of his life in Spain and died there after 405. Prudentius is closer to being a true Spaniard than the other Roman Spaniards. His poetry, although it kept the ancient quantitative meters of classical times, nevertheless dealt with subject matter that was, in part, Spanish. His *Cathemerinon* is a collection of twelve "hymns" too long for singing, appropriate for the various hours of the day. The *Peristephanon,* hymns about the crowns of martyrs (a number of them Spanish), is partly narrative and has been said to suggest antecedents of the later ballad form. He is thought of as one of the earliest and best Latin-Christian hymnologists and poets.

VISIGOTHIC SPAIN

Early in the fifth century the Visigoths entered Spain and conquered its Roman-Spanish inhabitants, all save a few cities in the south which were able for some years to claim allegiance to the Byzantine Empire. The Vandals had come to Spain shortly before the Visigoths, as had the Suevi and the Alans, but it was the Visigoths who made in Spain a kingdom for themselves. The Visigoths were not a numerous people (some authorities state that there were fewer than 300,000) and at first they were forbidden by their own laws to intermarry with the Hispano-Romans. Furthermore, they professed the Arian heresy, which greatly alienated them from their Roman Catholic subjects. It was not until the year 589 that one of their kings, Reccared, made the decision that made Roman Catholicism the religion of the Visigothic state. Thereafter

Spanish bishops held great authority, as much sometimes, and even more, than the Visigothic rulers themselves.

The Visigoths had lived in the Roman Empire and in association with the Romans long before they came to Spain. They were more than semicivilized, they borrowed much of Roman culture, their writing was in Latin, their laws a mingling of Visigothic custom law and of debased Roman law. The Visigothic period, however, was not one of great literary activity, and only a few names—one of these a truly great name—survive.

St. Isidore of Seville, or Isidorus Hispalensis (ca. 570-636) was the greatest writer of the entire period. He took an important and active part in the Arian controversy and succeeded his brother, St. Leander, as Bishop of Seville. His part in the councils that modified the Spanish Church was great. St. Isidore is best known for his efforts to preserve Greek and Latin learning from extinction. His greatest work, the *Etymologiae* (*Etymologies*) is a vast condensation of his incredibly wide reading in Greek and Latin and is a kind of encyclopedia of classical culture and knowledge. Its influence in Europe during his own time, and indeed throughout the Middle Ages and Renaissance, can hardly be overestimated. St. Isidore had many Spanish disciples.

Paulus Orosius (fifth-century native of Tarragona, probably) is credited with the first attempt to write a universal history. It was composed as a sort of apologia for Christianity and was called *Historiae Adversus Paganos* or *Books Against the Pagans,* of which there were seven.

MOORISH SPAIN

In the year 711 Moslems, indiscriminately called "Moors," invaded Spain from Africa and soon conquered the entire Peninsula except for a few valleys in Asturias, whose inhabitants were to make the beginnings of a reconquest. With the Arabs came eastern culture, a high civilization, eastern knowledge, sciences, music, arts, architecture—in short, an eastern way of life that left an indelible trace upon Spain and her people. A number of different dynasties ruled the land from 711 to 1492: the Abassids (711-756) ; the Ummayyads (756-1031) under whom Spanish Islam reached the peak of its grandeur and the splendid city of Cordova became the cultural equal of Damascus; the Almoravides (1086-1148) ; the Almohades (ca. 1148-1250); and the Nazarites or Alhamas of the Kingdom of Granada (1238-1492).

Europe recognized the excellence of Moorish Spain and its civilization, and many foreign Christian scholars studied there. Arab philosophers translated Aristotle and wrote commentaries on his works, thus introducing into the West much of lost Greek knowledge. To Moorish Spain came oriental literature:—tales, proverbs, themes and motifs, some from as far away as Persia and India. Under tolerant Moorish rule, the Jews became great scientists, philosophers, teachers, physicians, and writers. Both Jewish and Arabic poets flourished.

The contributions of Moorish Spain to Christian Spain and to the rest of Europe were great indeed, and if, as some scholars insist, these contributions were not original, they were none the less of great importance.

Arabic Writers

Mocádem of Cabra (near Cordova) was alive in 900 and was the first of the Spanish Arabs to compose verse in the form called *Muashaha*. (See Lyric Poetry in the Eleventh Century.)

Ibn Hazm (994-1063) is most noted for his *The Dove's Neckring*, a treatise on love in most of its phases. There is a sprinkling of poetry in the book. Ibn Hazm also wrote a comparative history of religion, a work of some value, in that it shows the sentiments of a rather critical and skeptical mind among the Spanish Moslems.

Ibn Zaydun of Cordova (1003-1070) wrote classical Arabic poems. His love affair with the Princess Wallada inspired the poetry, sometimes regarded as the most famous of Spanish-Arabic verse.

Ibn Guzman (d. 1160) of Cordova, like many other poets under the Taifa kings, wrote for a living. He used the *zéjel* (poems written in popular, not erudite, Arabic) on light themes, but for cultivated audiences rather than for the common people. He wrote on love, and he is a festive poet, singing the joys of wine, women, and song. Some see in his *zéjels* characteristics seen also in Provençal poetry, and there are scholars who believe that Provencal poetry of the trou-

badours was influenced by the poems of this and other
Spanish Moslems.

Arabic Spanish writers were very numerous in all areas of
literature and the sciences: travelers, physicians, agronomists,
map-makers, astronomers, historians, grammarians, writers of
fiction, and philosophers abounded.

Avempace (Abu Bakr Muhammad ibn Yahya) was one of
the earliest and the most distinguished of philosophers in
Moorish Spain. He was born (probably at Saragossa) in the
late eleventh century and excelled as a student of the exact
sciences and in poetry. His fame rests upon his philosophical
works, for he was a great thinker, a skeptic, and it is even
said that he rejected the Koran and believed that for mankind nothing existed beyond the grave. Of the twenty-five
works attributed to him only a few are extant. He greatly
influenced Averroes.

Averroes (1126-1198) was the greatest of Arabic philosophers in the West. He enjoyed the favor of two successive
Moorish rulers and rose to positions of great importance,
of which he complained because they made inroads upon his
hours of study. Later, at a time when speculative philosophy
was suspect, he was imprisoned, though he was finally freed.
In the Arabic world he is not famous, but among Christians
he is, for he wrote the most valued and famous commentaries
on the works of Aristotle, studies which focused the minds
of western schoolmen upon Greek philosophy, long fallen
into decay. His influence upon medieval philosophy was
enormous, and his works were translated out of Arabic and
into Latin, in which language they were read assiduously.

Moorish Spain, because the Moors were for a long time
tolerant of men of other faiths, produced many important
Jewish scholars, and some of the best translators were Jews.
Jews later translated for Spanish kings (Alfonso X, for
example) and Jewish physicians and financial experts served
at the courts of various Spanish kings and noblemen.

Maimonides of Cordova (Rabbi Moses ben Maimon,
1135-1204) was driven from Moorish Spain by the intolerant
Almohades. He went to Fez, and finally to Cairo, where he
was recognized as the greatest Rabbinic authority of his day.
Among his other activities, he served as physician to the famous
Saladin. As a philosopher he tried to reconcile Biblical and
Rabbinic teaching with philosophy, especially with the phi-

losophy of Aristotle. *The Guide for Those Who Have Lost Their Way* is his greatest masterpiece. His works were important during the Middle Ages and were printed in the Renaissance.

THE SPANISH LANGUAGE

Spanish is one of the Romance languages, and of the ten considered as Romance, it is spoken by the largest number of people. Its speakers, numbering far more than a hundred million, live in widely separated places: Spain, Spanish America (Portuguese is the language of Brazil), the Philippines, parts of Africa, the Balearic Islands, the Canaries, and by Spanish Jews in such places as Holland, Turkey, Africa and certain cities in the United States. Thousands of speakers of Spanish live in Texas, Colorado, New Mexico, California, and Arizona.

The Latin brought to Spain in the second century B.C. by Roman legions was not the polished literary Latin (*urbanitas*) of the Eternal City: rather it was the Latin spoken by the middle and lower classes, a speech sometimes called Vulgar Latin (*sermo vulgaris*). It was far less grammatical than the Latin of Cicero and Caesar. Its speakers had to some degree reduced the complicated case and declension systems of classic Latin, which was, after all, school Latin modeled to no small extent upon Greek grammar. The Latin verbal system, too complicated for the vulgar speaker, was considerably altered and new Romance tenses were developed to replace difficult Latin tenses (the Romance compound tenses developed in this way). The way in which words were pronounced by the man on the street was at variance with the Latin of the schools. Vulgar speakers replaced the classic quantitative system of vowel stress of long and short vowels with a qualitative stress of close and open vowels, leading to the development in Spanish of new diphthongs (*focum > fuego*) ; hiatus, so much a part of erudite Latin, broke down, allowing the formation of new diphthongs, which in turn led to the production of a number of startling changes in pronunciation (*filium > filyo > hijo*) ; the voicing of intervocalic consonants caused still other changes (*lupum > lobo*) ; the dropping of voiced consonants brought about still others (*amavi > amai > amé*). These and many other changes in sound and structure put Vulgar Latin on the road to what would lead in a few centuries to the birth of new Romance languages, including, of course, Spanish.

In Spain the Roman conquerors and later Roman settlers found a native population made up of several distinct groups. Iberians, Celts, Basques, and other peoples not yet well defined, attempted to speak Latin and altered it even further. The so-called substrata languages probably had a good deal to do with giving Spanish its distinctive character. Other factors leading to change were due to non-Roman members of the legions: Scythians, Syrians, Egyptians, Gauls, Germans, etc.

Basque, which is not a Romance language, had some slight influence upon the development of Spanish.

When the Visigoths invaded Spain in the early fifth century they found a Romanized land of Latin speakers whose tongue was readily understandable to other Latin speakers in different parts of the Empire. The Visigoths themselves, although a Germanic people, knew Latin, their records were kept in that language, and their native speech was certainly colored by Latin.

With the coming of the Visigoths came the beginning of what we call the Dark Ages, although in southern Spain, where Roman cities managed to exist and pay their allegiance to the Eastern Empire of Byzantium, Roman culture and Roman ways lingered on longer than in other parts of the fallen Empire.

Just when the spoken Latin of Spain drifted far enough from its earlier form to become a different language, Spanish, is not precisely known. Scholars believe that this took place in the sixth or seventh centuries, and that during this period it became difficult, and even impossible, for a Spaniard to cross the Pyrenees into France and make himself understood, for by then the Latin of France had drifted also into the beginnings of Old French. Once this had happened the Romance languages had arrived and Latin had died except for scholars and bookmen.

Of Visigothic hardly a trace remains, and what Germanic words came into Spanish probably came with the Romans themselves, who had adopted such Germanic words. This is true, too, to some degree with Celtic, a language that has left little but place names and a few nouns doubtless brought by the Romans into Spain from other Celtic areas. It was Latin, then, almost exclusively that produced Spanish.

With the coming of the Moors and Arabs in the early eighth century, Spanish, by then definitely a language in its own right, received rather a large body of new words, principally in the lexicographical areas of architecture, agriculture, warfare, and the sciences. But Spanish, even under Arabic domination, continued to be essentially a Latin language. Its very being and make-up were Latin. Arabic, aside from adding a fairly large vocabulary, did not change it.

Spanish has also at various times adopted words from still other languages: French, English, German, and even more. The discovery of the New World added thousands of words of unknown animals, plants, and objects.

Castilian, or Spanish, is then the dominant language of the Peninsula. Two other Romance languages are native to Spain. The northeastern region around Barcelona, Catalonia, speaks Catalan, which resembles Provençal more than it does Castilian. Valencian, spoken south of Catalonia, is a dialect of Catalan.

A third Romance language spoken in the Peninsula is that of Portugal: Portuguese, of which a dialect, Galician, is spoken in northwestern Spain (Galicia). Practically all those people living in any of the fifty Spanish provinces (and in Andorra) use Spanish in addition to any native dialect.

Surviving manuscripts prove that Spanish was quite adequate for literary expression in the eleventh and twelfth centuries. It has with time grown to be a constantly richer instrument.

The Eleventh and Twelfth Centuries

LYRIC POETRY	NARRATIVE POETRY	DRAMA	LAW–HISTORY	PROSE FICTION
Jarchas	*Juglaría* poetry (Epics):	*Auto de los Reyes Magos*	*Forum Judicum*	**Brief Narrative:**
Galician-Portuguese lyrics and popular Castilian songs	*Poema de Mio Cid* (ca. 1140)		*Historia Silense*	*Disciplina Clericalis* (ca. 1106)
	Roncesvalles (mid-twelfth century)		*Chronica Najerense*	
	<u>Lost Epics:</u>		*Historia Roderici*	
	Bernardo del Carpio		*Fueros* of the Visigoths	
	Los siete infantes de Lara or *Salas*			
	Gesta de Sancho II or *Cerco de Zamora*			

CHAPTER 2

The Eleventh and Twelfth Centuries

Reigns of: Ferdinand I (1035-1065) ; Sancho II (1065-1072) ; Alfonso VI (1072-1109) ; Doña Urraca (1109-1126) ; Alfonso VII (1126-1157) ; Sancho III (1157-1158) ; Alfonso VIII (1158-1214)

It was during the tenth century that Castile became an independent county under the rule of the famous count Fernán González (by 950). In the eleventh century Ferdinand I was crowned Castile's first king. When he fell heir to the kingdom of León, he became the first king of the two kingdoms. On his death the kingdoms suffered great confusion because his sons and daughters claimed the respective parts of the realm bequeathed them in Ferdinand's will. Castile went to Sancho; Galicia to García; León to Alfonso; and the cities of Toro and Zamora to the daughters Elvira and Urraca. Sancho II tried to seize all the territory for himself, but was murdered at Zamora during the siege, and Alfonso VI gained the power and unified the divided realm.

The eleventh century saw the fall of Toledo (1085) to Alfonso's troops, the capture of Valencia by the Cid, and the continuation of the Reconquest which would not end until 1492 with the fall of Granada to Ferdinand and Isabella. The Cid, Ruy Díaz de Bivar, stands as the great hero of the age.

During the eleventh century the monks of Cluny entered Spain, bringing the learning for which they were famous. Important also was the fall of the Caliphate of Cordova to the Almoravides. Moorish Spain had reached the peak of its culture and magnificence under the Caliphs of Cordova.

The twelfth century was not a period conducive to literature. The Kingdoms of Castile and León, divided by Ferdinand among his children, was the source of war and confusion. Alfonso VI and Alfonso VII continued the endless Reconquest, and out of the warfare between Moor and Christian came the famous epic *Poema de Mío Cid,* the great literary masterpiece of the century.

During this period the warrior monks of Islam, known as the Almoravides, defeated Alfonso VI and founded a strong realm in southern Spain. The Kingdom of Castile, in spite of defeat, continued to expand.

Spain's great military orders, founded to protect pilgrims and to wage war against the Moslem, came into being in the twelfth century: Calatrava (1158), Alcántara (1166), and Santiago (1175). Portugal's independence from León was recognized in 1143.

THE ELEVENTH CENTURY

Lyric Poetry

At least as early as the mid-eleventh century there existed a kind of early Spanish lyric poetry in Andalusia, and probably in other parts of Spain. Proof of this lies in the *jarchas.* Jewish and Arabic poets, who wrote a kind of poetry called *muashaha* in either five or six stanzas of Hebrew and dealing with themes traditional to this poetry, were in the habit of including a final stanza called a *jarcha* in Mozarabic Spanish. These *jarchas* were early Spanish folk poetry of a type later called *villancicos.* The fact that the Spanish words were written in Hebrew or in Arabic characters concealed the true nature of the *jarchas* for many years. Recently as many as fifty such poems have been discovered, many of true lyric freshness, proving conclusively that Spain had a lyric poetry long before the times of Berceo, and even before the schools of Galician-Portuguese poets. These *jarchas* may well be the oldest extant lyric poetry in medieval Europe, for they antedate the poems of William IX of Aquitaine (or William VII of Poitiers, as he is sometimes called), called the first of the troubadours.

It should be remembered that the *jarchas* were written in Arabic or Romance (the early Spanish of the eleventh and twelfth centuries), that they were love poems put into the mouths of women, although the poems were written by men, and that they are similar in form and manner of presentation to the early *villancicos* and *estribillos*. Indeed, Spanish *coplas* sung to this day bear a close resemblance to the early *jarchas*.

Narrative Poetry

Narrative folk poetry, particularly of the sort that is found in the heroic poems of the Germanic peoples, may have existed among the Visigoths who overran Spain in the early fifth century. Such popular poetry probably survived, especially in areas not under Moorish control, but none has survived from a period earlier than the twelfth century.

THE TWELFTH CENTURY

Lyric Poetry

No Castilian lyric poetry, as distinct from the *jarcha* of Southern Spain, has survived from the twelfth century. The Mozarabs, Spaniards living under Moorish rule, probably continued the popular poetry they had been using in the eleventh century. In the northwest, Galician-Portuguese poetry, some probably from folk tradition and some modeled upon the poetry of the troubadours of Provence, was beginning to flower, but it was not to reach the peak of its development for another century. It is quite possible, too, that in the north native and popular poetry of some sort existed beside the poetry borrowed from the troubadours.

Narrative Poetry

Mester de juglaría, 'the minstrels' poetry,' was used for epics as well as for other narrative poems in the thirteenth century. This form of poetry was characterized by lines of irregular length, averaging 16 syllables (although some had as many as 20) broken in the middle by a caesura, or pause. There was assonance rather than full rhyme. All this poetry in the twelfth century is anonymous, even though it reached its peak in this period.

The *Poema de Mío Cid,* most famous of the Spanish epics, was composed around 1140 (perhaps somewhat later), but the sole surviving manuscript was copied by a scribe named Per Abbat in 1307. The *Poema* was first published in modern times by Tomás Antonio Sánchez in 1779, and contains some 3700 lines. Based upon the life of Rodrigo Díaz de Bivar, who died in 1099, the poem is realistic, although it incorporates certain fictitious elements. In tone, presentation, and subject matter the *Poema* differs greatly from the highly imaginative French *chanson de geste*. It is divided into three cantos: in Canto I the Cid (the Arabic *Sidi* means 'my lord') , so named by his allies among the Moslems, is exiled by Alfonso VI, and marches east with a conquering army through Moorish Spain; Canto II tells of the Cid's capture of Moorish Valencia (historically accurate) and of the marriage of his daughters (legendary) to the Infantes de Carrión, who turn out to be great cowards; Canto III deals with the affront to the Cid's daughters by their husbands and of the trial by combat between the husbands and the Cid's champions. The style of the *Poema* is terse, but the story moves and sustains interest. The Cid was a hero of the people; his story is told realistically and simply by someone who lived in, or not long after, those times.

Roncesvalles, written in the mid-twelfth century, shows the influence of the *chanson de geste*. Only 100 lines have survived, but it is apparent that these once belonged to a longer poem. In moving and vivid realism this fragment tells of the extreme grief of Charlemagne upon seeing the remains of his slaughtered army at the Battle of Roncesvalles in 778, when Saracens (actually Basques) ambushed and destroyed the French host as it was returning from the siege of Saragossa. Of high emotional quality is the king's sorrow on finding the bodies of Roland and Oliver.

The lost epics of the thirteenth century, the existence of which is indicated in the prose chronicles of the thirteenth century, are of some importance, at least in subject matter: (1) *Rodrigo el Godo,* the story of the last king of the Visigoths, who lost his realm to the Moslems; (2) *Bernardo del Carpio,* the story of a fictitious Leonese hero of the eighth century; (3) *Los siete infantes de Lara* or *Salas,* the account of a feud, the murder of seven brothers, and the vengeance taken by a half-brother named Mudarra; (4) *El Cerco de Zamora,* which reports the events of the siege of Zamora by Sancho II and of this king's murder by Bellido Dolfos.

The Drama

No survival of drama before the late twelfth or early thirteenth century has come down to us. Both lay and church drama, however, are known to have existed in France, and in thirteenth century Spain laws were written to regulate theatrical productions. These laws were the *Siete Partidas* of King Alfonso X (see Alfonsine writings in the thirteenth century).

The *Auto de los Reyes Magos,* a short drama preserved in an incomplete manuscript of 147 lines, probably from the late twelfth century, is the only surviving play from this period. It belongs to the well-known Nativity Cycle, and relates the travels of the Magi, their meeting, their arrival at the court of Herod, and the concern of the king of the Hebrews over the news of the birth of the Savior. The little play is filled with action and dramatic force, and there are touches of humor and some good characterization.

Law

Visigothic or custom law, existed from early times. The largest such code was the *Forum Judicum (Law of the Judges),* later called the *Fuero Juzgo.* This code was written in Latin and was the most important source of later Spanish Law. Based upon a mixture of debased Roman law and the custom law of the Visigoths, it stands as the first great compilation of Spanish jurisprudence.

History

The *Historia Silense* (1115) was an early attempt to write history and not merely annals; *Chronica Najerense* (ca. 1160) used poetic sources for history of the eleventh and twelfth centuries in Spain; *Historia Roderici* narrated some of the exploits of the Cid; the *Liber Chronicorum* of Bishop Pelayo of Oviedo (ca. 1132) was also famous. All of these, as their titles suggest, were written in Latin.

Prose Fiction

The *Disciplina Clericalis (Scholar's Guide) of* **Petrus Alfonsi** (Pedro Alfonso) is Spain's contribution to prose fiction in the twelfth century. The author, known also by his Jewish name of Moses Sephardi, was baptized in 1106 with his principal sponsor in baptism the King of Aragon, Alfonso I, the Battler. His *Disciplina* was in some ways one of the most important books in the Middle Ages. It is a collection of oriental short stories or apologues, known in those times as *exempla,* and it is the first such group of stories translated into a western language, in this case Latin. It introduced into Europe many eastern tales, some of which are among the world's best-known stories, and it did a great deal to shape the subsequent development of fiction in Europe. Proverbs and maxims appear also, and the *Disciplina Clericalis* may be considered as one of the earliest translations of such pithy eastern sayings. The book had a didactic purpose certainly, for the twelfth century was an age of didacticism, but there was a recreational intent also, to judge from the subject matter of some of the stories whose morals are often hardly justified.

The Thirteenth Century

The Thirteenth Century

LYRIC POETRY	NARRATIVE POETRY	THEATER	LAW AND HISTORY	DIDACTIC WORKS	NARRATIVE PROSE
The Galician-Portuguese Lyric:	Mester de Juglaría (non epic):	See Siete Partidas (Law)	Fuero Juzgo (1241)	Flores de Filosofía	Calila y Dimna
Cántigas de Santa María of Alfonso X	Disputa del alma y el cuerpo		Setenario	Libro de los buenos proverbios	Libro de los engaños (1253)
Some 2000 poems in Galician-Portuguese gathered together into three great books.	Denuestos del agua y el vino		Las Siete Partidas (1256–1265)	Bonium or Bocados de Oro	Barlaan y Josaphat
	Elena y María		Lucas of Tuy, Chronicum Mundi (1236)	Libro de los doce sabios	Historia troyana (1270)
The Castilian Lyric	Santa María Egipcíaca Libro de los tres reyes de Oriente		Rodrigo of Toledo, De Rebus Hispaniae (ca. 1237)	Poridad de poridades	
Eya velar, a watchman's song in Berceo's Duelo de la Virgen.	Mester de Clerecía: Poema de Fernán González		Primera Crónica General or Historia de España (Alfonso X, ca. 1280)	Alfonsine works: Tablas Alfonsíes (1262–1272)	
Razón de amor	Libro de Alexandre		General Historia (Alfonso X, ca 1280)	Libros del saber de Astronomía (1276–1279)	
	Libro de Apolonio			Liber Picatrix (1256)	
	Works of Gonzalo de Berceo			Libro de ajedrez, dados y tablas	
				Setenario	
				Lapidarios (ca. 1275)	

CHAPTER 3

The Thirteenth Century

Reigns of: Henry I (1214-1217); Alfonso IX of León (1188-1230); Ferdinand III (1230-1252); Alfonso X (1252-1284); Sancho IV (1284-1295); Ferdinand IV (1295-1312).

This was an important century for Spain. The two great kingdoms of Castile and León were united under Ferdinand III, called "el Santo." Moorish Spain was greatly reduced by this monarch. Cordova, Seville, Murcia fell to his armies, and by and large, the power of the Moors was broken, for only in the Kingdom of Granada did they hold firm. Ferdinand had the *Forum Judicum* rendered into Spanish as the *Fuero Juzgo*.

His son, Alfonso X, called "el Sabio," although not so much a warrior and a politician as Ferdinand, was nevertheless in many ways even more important. He is remembered for his patronage of the arts and sciences, of music and literature, and for his efforts to have the extant knowledge of the realm translated into Spanish for all his subjects to use. His school of translators (Spanish Jews for the most part) translated much from Arabic. Spanish learning in the century centered around the court of this king. Spanish law to this day owes its being to his code of laws. Under his patronage Spain had her first important histories in Spanish, and Spanish music owes much of its early development to his support. His rule has been regarded as a kind of thirteenth-century renaissance.

King Alfonso's unfortunate efforts to have himself elected Emperor of the Holy Roman Empire and his troubles with rebellious nobles and with his son, Sancho IV, "el Bravo,"

are more than overbalanced by his contributions to his
country's culture and knowledge.

POETRY

The Galician-Portuguese Lyric

It is quite likely that the lyric tradition represented by
the *jarchas* survived and flourished in all parts of the Peninsula, but the bulk of poems which have actually survived
in written form come from Galician-Portuguese territory.
Most of these poems were modeled on those of the Provençal
troubadours, and most are aristocratic rather than popular in
inspiration. Even Castilian poets wrote their lyrics in Galician-
Portuguese down to the fifteenth century. More than 2000
such songs composed by 200 named poets—kings, noblemen,
and a few commoners—survive in three great song books, now
referred to as *Cancioneiro da Ajuda, Cancioneiro Português
da Vaticana,* and *Cancioneiro Colocci-Brancuti.* Of the three
classes of songs composed, the *Cántigas de escarnio* are songs
of vilification and abuse, often quite scurrilous; the *cántigas
de amor* are rather conventional love songs; and the *cántigas
de amigo,* put in the mouth of the lovelorn lass and far the
most attractive of the group, often breathed real lyric freshness
and may come from popular origins. The Galician-Portuguese
school of poets lasted for about a century and a half after
1200. It is never to be forgotten that all these early poems
were written to be sung, and not for reading in the studies
of scholars.

The *Cántigas de Santa María* were written partly by, and
partly for, King Alfonso X, el Sabio, who ruled Castile and
León 1252-1284 and who was the most fertile poet in Galician-
Portuguese. The *Cántigas* contain more than 400 poems that
sing the miracles of the Holy Virgin. The sources are the
great Latin collections of miracles known all over Europe
as well as Spanish tradition and folklore. The manuscripts of
the *Cántigas* are important also as early Spanish art works,
for the miracles are illustrated by beautiful miniatures. These
pictures furnish also a vivid picture of the daily life in
Alfonso's reign. Each miracle is a song with accompanying
verses and musical scores. The music of the Gregorian chant
is the basis for some of the songs, while others come from

the folk songs of Spain, possibly even from Arabic-Spanish songs.

The Castilian Lyric

Only a few poems of lyric nature might be traced from the thirteenth century, although there is a strong probability that much folk poetry existed. The people who wrote books of poetry were the educated, and they preferred Galician-Portuguese verse to Castilian, and in general preferred erudite rather than popular forms.

The *Razón de amor,* an anonymous Castilian lyric, probably early thirteenth century, contains elements of Aragonese dialect. Its subject, the meeting of two lovers in a beautiful setting, follows to some degree the Galician variety of love poem and contains a good deal of symbolism and allegory. The versification is irregular and is based principally upon lines of 8 and 9 syllables. Attached to it appears a debate in verse entitled *Denuestos del agua y el vino,* which is more in the spirit of narrative poetry than lyric.

Castilian Narrative Poetry. *Mester de Juglaría*

Narrative verse in the *mester de juglaría* continued in the thirteenth century, although the old epic themes fell into some disuse. Instead there were disputes and saints' lives. These poems are usually in rhymed couplets and verses of 8 syllables, although there is some irregularity in this respect. Disputes (*débats*) were popular in France, and were probably borrowed from that country by Spanish writers.

The *Disputa del alma y el cuerpo,* probably of Anglo-Norman origin, was written in couplets of 7 and 8 syllable lines. The soul takes the body to task for the wicked life it has led. *Los denuestos del agua y el vino,* attached to the lyric *Razón de amor,* is a dispute between water and wine, each of which argues its own virtues. The lines are irregular rhymed couplets. Still another poem of the same category is *Elena y María.* Elena's lover is a knight and María's a cleric. Each girl states the virtues of her innamorato, and the cleric (scholar) wins, for after all, a cleric wrote the poem. The rhymed couplets in octosyllabic verses are colored by Leonese dialect.

Santa María Egipcíaca, a long narrative saint's life, recounts the life of María, the courtesan of Alexandria, before she was converted, as well as after, when she did penance in the wilderness. Modeled upon a French original, the Castilian version shows some traces of originality and makes interesting reading. There is a mixture of 8- and 9-syllable lines.

The *Libro de los tres reyes de Oriente* is a poem of 250 lines that relates the arrival of the Magi, the Slaughter of the Innocents, the Flight into Egypt, and the story of the two thieves, Gestas and Dimas. Eight-syllable lines predominate, but there are some of 9.

Castilian Narrative Poetry. *Mester de Clerecía*

In the thirteenth century and in the fourteenth the *mester de clerecía* (scholar's poetry) flourished. It was characterized by monorhymed quatrains rather than assonance, regular lines of 14 syllables with a caesura or pause in the middle of each. This poetry is also known as *cuaderna vía* (the fourfold way).

The *Poema de Fernán González* is the only poem that has survived using epic material and written in *cuaderna vía*. Fernán González (d. 970) was the founder of Castilian independence. The poem was written about 1250 and relates the wonderful, yet realistic events connected with this count's conquests for Castile.

The *Libro de Apolonio,* which was written during the first half of the thirteenth century, is the first appearance of a Byzantine tale to emerge in Spanish. Based probably upon a lost Greek novel, it is more romantic and less heroic than *Fernán González*. In 2624 lines it tells the story of Apollonius, King of Tyre, who finds his lost daughter Tarsiana after shipwrecks, separations, and strange adventures. The exact source of the Spanish version is not known, but its author might have drawn from the Latin or French redactions which were available to him. The book had great influence in Europe and appeared in most of the vernacular literatures in the Middle Ages. Like so many books in thirteenth-century Spain, the *Libro de Apolonio* drew from oriental tales.

Gonzalo de Berceo (b. late 12th century) was the first Castilian poet known by name. He is more famous for his narrative verse in the *mester de clerecía* than for anything else, although he includes a short lyric poem in his *Duelo de la Virgen,* itself a narrative poem. A watchman's song appears in the *Duelo* and its title is *Eya velar*. In short lines, in all probability of popular origin, this soldiers' or watchmen's song is quite likely not to be Berceo's creation.

His greatest literary activity was between 1220 and 1242, and almost all of his poetry is of a religious nature. A simple and earthy person, he presents in great detail a picture of the life of his times among the peasants and common people.

The *Milagros de Nuestra Señora,* his best-known work, recounts a series of 25 miracles wrought by the Virgin Mary and includes some of the most famous of such miracles, which Berceo drew from the common fund distributed throughout Europe. The miracles are written in a simple and often quaint way, and some modern critics consider Berceo a good example of a poet of considerable primitive charm.

Other saints' lives written by Berceo are *Vida de Santo Domingo de Silos, Vida de San Millán,* and *Vida de Santa Oria,* all of which deal with Spanish saints. These saints' lives depict life in Berceo's Spain. Other poems written by this fertile cleric are the *Martirio de San Lorenzo, Loores de Nuestra Señora, Duelo de la Virgen, Sacrificio de la Misa,* and the *Signos del Juicio.*

The *Libro de Alexandre* of the mid-thirteenth century contains 10,500 lines and was written by a poet of considerable culture and education. He could hardly have been a simple priest like Berceo. The book portrays Alexander the Great as the perfect medieval knight, draws heavily upon the knowledge surviving from the ancient world, and inserts so much information that it is a veritable encyclopedia of medieval knowledge. Geography, history, astronomy, customs of men, and habits of beasts all went into it. The author, not content to deal with the life of Alexander, relates apologues and fables, includes letters supposedly exchanged between famous personages (for example Aristotle and Alexander), inserts long didactic passages, and presents allegorical treatments of many subjects. The book represents the urge of thirteenth-century man to teach and to offer all in the way of knowledge that was available to him.

THE THEATER

No survivals of Spanish drama have been found in this century, but there is evidence to support the statement that several varieties of plays existed. Since King Alfonso's *Siete*

Partidas, a great code of laws, regulate drama, it is thereby proved that there were both secular and clerical plays, given inside the church and outside it, that actors might be either clerics or laymen, and that some plays required paid admission. The laws show alarm at *juegos de escarnio,* scurrilous dramas in which the clergy might be ridiculed. The famous mystery play, still given at the Mediterranean town of Elche, may be the descendant of some of the early church dramas.

ALFONSINE LEARNING

King Alfonso X (1252-1284) was known as el Sabio (the Learned), and not without cause. His rule has been considered as a kind of thirteenth-century renaissance, for under his patronage the arts and sciences flourished in Spain as never before. In some ways he was one of the most important men of the Middle Ages.

Law

King Alfonso's code of laws, called the *Siete Partidas* from its seven parts, was put together between 1256 and 1265, although it was not promulgated until 1348 in the times of Alfonso XI. It drew from the Code of Justinian, the many *fueros* (charters and privileges), and from a number of didactic works. The *Forum Judicum (Laws of the Judges)* compiled at the order of Ferdinand III, the *Setenario* (at least in part a rough draft of the *Partidas),* and the *Fuero Real* (ca. 1255) were among the codes of law that contributed to the *Partidas,* which furnish one of the most complete pictures of medieval life among all classes of people. All phases of law are covered, clerical as well as secular, and even though not promulgated the *Partidas* seem to have served as a guide to existing law and as a basis for subsequent legal treatises.

History

Before the writing of King Alfonso's histories, Spanish historians had written in Latin. **Lucas of Tuy,** called 'el Tudense,' had written his *Chronicum Mundi* (ca. 1236) for the wife of Alfonso IX. It dealt with the Visigothic period and recounted for the most part the history of Castile and León during the Reconquest. **Rodrigo de Toledo** wrote the first great history of the Spanish Middle Ages. His *De Rebus*

Hispaniae, written in Latin also, treats the history of the Visigothic peoples before their entry into Spain and after, with the Moorish Conquest and the affairs of Asturias, Castile, and León.

Two great historical works of the thirteenth century were written under the patronage of Alfonso X. The *(Primera) Crónica General* or *Historia de España* was planned as a history of Spain from the earliest times until the death of Ferdinand III (1252). Sources are the Bible, the Spanish epics, Arabic historians, and such Spanish historians as Lucas of Tuy and Rodrigo de Toledo, as well as a good deal of purely fictional material, no doubt regarded in those times as factual. The work marks the turning point in historical writing in Spain and was the source of many later histories.

The *Grande y General Historia* (ca. 1280) was planned as a history of the world from the Creation to the times of Alfonso himself, but it reached no further than the birth of Jesus. It was a kind of paraphrase of the Vulgate Old Testament, mixed with mythology and the history of the ancient world (Greece, Egypt, Rome).

Scientific Works

King Alfonso was so interested in the sciences, especially astronomy, that he was sometimes called 'el estrellero' (the star-gazer). His *Tablas Alfonsies (Alfonsine Tables)* were translated from the Arabic and deal with the movements of the planets as based upon the findings of the Arabic astronomer al-Zarqali. The *Tablas* enjoyed great fame during the Middle Ages and the Renaissance.

The *Libros del Saber de Astronomia* were translated from the Arabic or were based upon Arabic works from the ninth to the twelfth centuries. The *Libros* are divided into 15 treatises on the cataloguing of the stars and the construction of astronomical instruments. They were written between 1276 and 1279.

The *Liber Picatrix,* dealing mainly with magic, was translated in Alfonso's court.

The *Libro de Ajedrez, Dados, y Tablas* is a book on chess, backgammon, and other games and was translated from Arabic about 1260. Numerous illustrations show the players, most of whom are Moorish.

The famous *Lapidary,* as we know the book in English

terminology, was written during the last ten years of Alfonso's reign (d. 1284). There may possibly have been earlier transcriptions. It is a translation from works in Arabic and it describes the virtues of stones, tells where they are to be found, speaks of the influence of the stars upon the stones and of the power stones impart to the people who wear them. One may read in the *Lapidario* of such remarkable stones as the "stone that flies from wine" which leaps away from vessels containing alcoholic liquids, or of the "stone of sleep," much prized by surgeons as an anesthetic. A great store of medieval eastern lore is to be found in these chapters.

PROVERBIAL WORKS

Proverbs and maxims were of great interest to the people of this period, especially those books that used as their sources the great collections of the East. A good many such eastern books were translated into Spanish, although some came by way of Latin instead of Arabic. Four of the important Spanish collections of proverbs are the following: (1) the *Flores de filosofía,* which is divided into 39 chapters and claims to be the wisdom of 37 sages, including Seneca; (2) the *Libro de los buenos proverbios,* like some other collections, was first written in Greek and later rendered into Arabic, making it an important mingling of Greek philosophy and oriental wisdom; (3) the *Bonium* or *Bocados de oro,* an adaptation from an Arabic work containing two spurious letters attributed to Alexander the Great, is named for Bonium, the imaginary sage whose wisdom is presented; (4) the *Poridad de poridades,* sometimes known as the *Castigos de Aristótil y Alexandre,* is a translation of the *Secreta Secretorum,* a well known Latin version of this material.

PROSE FICTION

The narrative of the period was made up principally of translations from well-known oriental collections of tales, some having originated in the Near East (Hebrew, Arabic, Syriac tales) and some in Persia and India. These tales, carried westward, eventually were set down in Arabic or Hebrew, and it is from these languages that they entered Spanish, especially from Arabic. Their entry into Spain was important to western letters, for they brought to Europe many new tales, plots, and themes and in time formed the background of a great part of western story.

Calila y Dimna was translated from Arabic in 1251, some believe at the command of Alfonso X. This was the first book of oriental tales to appear in Spanish. It can be traced back through Arabic and Persian to the materials found in the Hindu *Panchatantra (Five Books of Tales)*. *Calila y Dimna* brought into Spanish some of the world's great stories and fables and introduced to western readers new techniques of telling stories.

The *Libro de los engaños y asayamientos de las mujeres,* translated from the Arabic in 1253 at the behest of Prince Fadrique, brother of Alfonso X, is a Spanish version of the *Book of Sindibad* (not to be confused with Sinbad the Sailor in the *Arabian Nights*). Elements from a number of oriental sources make up the book, and these, together with the entertaining frame story and the many spicy tales of wicked women, gave it great popularity. English readers know it best under the title of the *Book of the Seven Sages,* but the Spanish version is more lively and interesting and much closer to the oriental original. Literally scores of books in Europe felt the influence of the *Book of Sindibad,* although not always through the Spanish, of course. It is still savored by all those who love naughty and clever stories.

Barlaam y Josaphat, known widely in the thirteenth century through the Latin version found in the *Speculum Historiale* of Vicent of Beauvais, was originally an oriental work, a Christian version of the life of the Buddha. The work, as it appeared in Greek, is attributed to St. John of Damascus, and it was from the Greek that the story made its way into European literature. The purpose of the book is didactic, its *exempla* are all pious, or at least ethical in nature; even so, it is well told, and its popularity in Spain, as well as in all Europe, was phenomenal. Some of the stories introduced into western literature were such famous themes as the 'three caskets' tale as used in *The Merchant of Venice.*

The *Historia troyana,* written about 1270, contains both verse and prose. It is a Spanish version of the French *Roman de Troie* of Benoît de Sainte-Maure and a fine example of the Cycle of Antiquity in medieval literature. Its source originally was probably the Greek tales fictitiously attributed to Dares and Dictys. These stories entered Spain also from the work of Guido della Colonna of the late thirteenth century.

The Fourteenth Century

The Fourteenth Century

LYRIC POETRY	NARRATIVE POETRY	THEATER	HISTORY	DIDACTIC WORKS	PROSE FICTION
Galician-Portuguese Lyric: Gonzalo Rodríguez Archdeacon of Toro. Macías el Enamorado (see 15th Century). Pero Ferrús or Ferránd (see *Cancionero de Baena*). Juan Ruiz, Archpriest of Hita: *Libro de buen amor.* (contains lyric poems). Garci Fernández de Jerena (1365–1400) Pero Vélez de Guevara (d. ca. 1420)	*Mester de Juglaría:* Lost Epics (see History) *Cantar de Rodrigo or Mocedades del Cid; Gesta de don Juan de Montemayor.* *Poema de Alfonso Onceno* *Mester de Clerecía:* *Poema de Yuçuf* (Aljamiada literature). *Proverbios del sabio Salomón* (See Didactic Literature) *Vida de San Ildefonso* Juan Ruiz, Archpriest of Hita: *Libro de buen amor* *Libro de miseria de omne* Pero López de Ayala *Rimado de palacio.*	No plays preserved	Fernán Sánchez de Valladolid (1313–1359), *Crónicas.* and *Crónica de Alfonso XI* (?) *Crónica rimada* *Gran Conquista de Ultramar* *Crónica de Alfonso XI* Juan Núñez de Villaizán Don Juan Manuel: *Crónica abreviada* (1320–1324) and *Crónica complida* (?) (1329) Pero López de Ayala: *Crónicas de los reyes de Castilla*	Poetry: *Proverbios del sabio Salomón.* (See Juglaría Poetry). Sem Tob: *Proverbios morales* (gnomic literature). Pedro de Veragüe, *La doctrina de la discrición.* Prose: Don Juan Manuel: *Libro del caballero et del escudero; Libro de los estados* (1326); *Libro de la caza* (1326); *Tractados de armas* (1332). Pero López de Ayala: *Libro de cetrería or de las aves de la caza;* translation—Livy, Boethius, Gregory, Isidore, Guido de Colonna, Boccaccio. Sancho IV: *Castigos y documentos* (See Prose)	Brief Narrative: Don Juan Manuel: *El Conde Lucanor* Sancho IV. *Castigos y documentos para bien vivir* (see didactic literature). Novelesque Prose: *El Caballero Cifar* (about 1300) *Amadís de Gaula* *La Doncella Teodor.* *Crónica Troyana* (not to be confused with 13th-century *Historia Troyana.* *La Gran Conquista de Ultramar*

CHAPTER 4

The Fourteenth Century

Reigns of: Ferdinand IV (1295-1310) ; Alfonso XI (1310-1350) ;
Peter I (1350-1369) ; Henry II (1369-1379) ; John I (1379-
1390) ; Henry III (1390-1406) .

This was a period of war and civil war, of political up-
heaval, and a continuation of the Reconquest. The study
of the arts and sciences, so avidly pursued by the scholars of
Alfonso X, waned. The Black Death struck Spain, just as it
struck the rest of Europe. The kings of Spain were not out-
standing patrons of literature. In spite of all this, literature
was written, and at least two writers have earned a place
among the immortals. One, a prince, Don Juan Manuel,
nephew of Alfonso X, wrote a collection of prose tales; the
other, a priest, Juan Ruiz, Archpriest of Hita, wrote the
perennially famous *Libro de buen amor.* The ruling house of
Trastamara made its beginning in the fourteenth century and
was to produce a number of kings, and in the fifteenth
century, the famous Isabella of Castile.

LYRIC POETRY

Poetry written in the Galician-Portuguese language continued to be in vogue among erudite poets, although Castilian
was coming into its own. The lyric in Galician still modeled
itself after the Provençal school, although folk or native
Spanish themes and ideas were included. A number of poets
who preferred Galician lived in the fourteenth century, but
are considered fifteenth century poets because their writings
appear in the fifteenth-century *Cancionero de Baena.* Among
these are **Macías, Garci Fernández de Jerena, Pero Ferrús**
or **Ferrández,** and **Pero Vélez de Guevara. Gonzalo Rodrí-**

guez, Archdeacon of Toro, who wrote between 1379 and 1390, composed verse in Castilian as well as in Galician. The greatest poet of the fourteenth century was **Juan Ruiz,** Archpriest of Hita, author of the famous *Libro de buen amor.* He regarded his book, which will be considered at greater length under narrative *clerecía* poetry, as a kind of *ars poetica* and used a wide variety of verse forms, some of which, like his own *serranillas,* appear to be forerunners of the *serranillas* of the following century. Some of his lyric poetry is of high quality.

Narrative Poetry: Juglaría

Interest in the epic did not die in the fourteenth century, although there was a considerable change in tone and a pulling away from the old epic formula of the *Poema de Mío Cid* (twelfth century) and the *Poema de Fernán González* (thirteenth century) which survived only in *clerecía.* The interest in the human aspects of the lives and characters of epic heroes brought about redactions of old themes and created new roles for these heroes. The *Mester de juglaría* gave way in this century before the *clerecía,* just as it had in the thirteenth.

The *Cantar de Rodrigo,* or *Mocedades del Cid,* was written in *juglaría* poetry, possibly as late as the early fifteenth century, but in tone it belongs to the fourteenth, if not even to earlier times. Its date of composition is usually given as 1400. The poem, an important redaction of epic material, gives a new character to the Cid, and shows him as a young man filled with vim, vigor, and even humor. Added to the material taken from historical sources is a great deal of folklore, legend, and tradition, and possibly even from the imagination of the redactor. It was this redaction and one in prose found in the *Crónica de 1344* (see History) plus certain ballads of the next century that served as the source of the *Cid* of Guillén de Castro and of Corneille, important developments of Spanish and French drama of the Golden Age (see Drama in 17th Century). It should be noted that the *Cantar de Rodrigo* forms a part (lines 280-1125) of a longer work, *La Crónica rimada de las cosas de España* (see History). The importance of these redactions of the Cid's life is great, because of their influence upon subsequent literature.

The *Poema de Alfonso Onceno* is a long (2455 stanzas)

historical poem dealing with the life and Moorish wars of King Alfonso XI (d. 1350) of Castile. It is realistic and filled with a great deal of daily life and customs of the time. The authorship has been attributed to a certain Ruy Yáñez, but scholars now believe that he was no more than a copyist. The poem may have come from a Portuguese original, for the lines, when rendered into Portuguese, make better poetry than the Spanish. The verse form is important, for it is regarded as a link between the epic meter of *juglaría* poetry and the ballad. Some regard it as verse of 18 syllables broken by a caesura with rhyme ABAB at the end of each hemistich; others prefer to think of it as two separate quatrains set side by side, each rhyming ABAB.

Narrative Poetry: Clerecía

The *Poema de Yuçuf* is an incomplete poem belonging to *aljamiada literature* (Spanish set down in Arabic characters), and is indeed taken from an Arabic source, which presents the story of Joseph in Egypt according to the version found in the *Koran*. It was written in strophes of *cuaderna vía* by an Aragonese Morisco in the fourteenth century, or possibly even in the thirteenth.

The *Proverbios del sabio Solomón* is an anonymous work that belongs to the tradition of *clerecía* poetry. The poem deals with the proverbs of Solomon and with their message. It has been attributed to Pero López de Ayala by reason of its severe tone. Still another poem in *clerecía* verse is a work known as the *Vida de San Ildefonso*. It treats the life of St. Ildefonso, Bishop of Toledo, and although of little literary interest, it throws some valuable light on modes of life in fourteenth-century Spain.

The greatest poet of the century and perhaps the greatest writer of the entire Spanish Middle Ages was **Juan Ruiz,** Archpriest of Hita. The reverend Juan Ruiz was a stout and sturdy fellow and even a sensual type, according to his own word portrait of himself. He loved rollicking companions, male and female, and wrote an extensive, vivid miscellany about them (maybe even more about himself) in vigorous and charming verse. He seems to have been born in the 1280's in Alcalá de Henares. He somehow managed to become Archpriest of Hita. For reasons unknown the stern Archbishop of Toledo, Don Gil de Albornoz, clapped him in

the ecclesiastical prisons (some scholars would vigorously
deny this) for thirteen years. Presumably he died a little before 1350. Most of what is known about him comes from
his own delightfully uninhibited and revealing work.

Juan Ruiz tells us more than once that he is championing
good love, that is, love of God and good works, spirituality,
as against worldly love or mad love *(loco amor)*, apparently
all too common in the fourteenth century. It is not difficult,
however, to see that his interest centers a good deal more on
the "mad" variety of the sentiment of love.

Juan Ruiz has been called "the Spanish Chaucer," although
his work is far more disconnected and varied than the *Canter-
bury Tales*. It is a vast hodge-podge of medieval lore held
together by the thin thread of narrative about a certain
Melón de la Huerta Ortiz. Three periods of Melón's (the
archpriest's?) life may be regarded as giving the book three
divisions. In the first the young Melón, inexperienced in love,
makes several failures in courtship; in the second part he is
instructed in both courtly and Ovidian love by Venus and
Cupid, and it is from these gods that he learns that he must
choose a go-between, the remarkable Trotaconventos, forerunner of the Celestina. Through this go-between he is able
to seduce Doña Endrina, whom he later marries. In the
last division the now-instructed Melón continues his love
affairs and completes the jolly dissection of medieval woman-
hood, begun early in the book.

The whole panorama of the fourteenth century is laid before the reader, and many social levels and professions are
described and satirized, for the most part with humorous
joviality. Juan Ruiz thought of his book, among other things
(see Lyric Poetry) as an art of poetry, but some think
he was writing a jolly treatise to initiate the middle class
and even the lower classes into the mysteries and joys of
Ovidian and courtly love. Ruiz' sources, aside from Ovid (in-
directly borrowed), were numerous—oriental tales, fabliaux,
Aesopic fables, French satirical themes *(Battle of Carnal and
Lent)*, Goliardic poems, medieval Latin plays and poems,
miracles of the Virgin, and the folklore of Spain, plus his own
experiences in life.

There is one spice that dominates and binds together this
medieval *potpourri*: the vividly arresting personality of Juan
Ruiz. His masterpiece is unquestionably one of the most

zestful and lively compositions to emerge from the Middle Ages anywhere. We are all the more impressed when we compare the archpriest's insouciant liveliness with the long-bearded gravity of his (far more aristocratic) contemporary Don Juan Manuel, and the somewhat later Pero López de Ayala. The *Book of Good Love* celebrates the triumph of the vital over the ascetic.

The sad *Libro de miseria de omne,* was probably written by a monk in the fourteenth century. It follows the *De Contemptu Mundi* of Innocent III (written when this pope was a young man), a collection of Biblical and profane treatises on the misery of mankind. The writer also included material from the lives of the saints. There is likewise a valuable treatment of the estates of society, with the author's opinion of each. The satire is keen, and appears to be that of a priest willing to condemn the upper classes.

Pero López de Ayala (1332-1407) wrote a long poem in *cuaderna vía,* the last great work in this type of poetry. His *Rimado de palacio* is a multiform poem held together only by the personality of the writer. The "religious part" treats such matters as the Ten Commandments and the Seven Deadly Sins; the social and political part deals with the affairs of the court, and is a biting and fierce satire against social evils; lyrics (such as hymns to the Virgin) are scattered throughout the *Rimado,* but these do not compare in excellence with those of the Archpriest of Hita. A third part might be the matter of Ayala's treatment of politics, of what the ideal government should be, and a broad and detailed description of society which gives a rather full picture of the ways of men in those times.

As a historian López de Ayala ranks highest in his century. He took an active part in politics, served as official historian to four kings, whose *Crónicas* he wrote: Peter the Cruel, Henry II, John I, and Henry III, covering the years 1350-1406. He based his writings on observation and he wrote realistically. The *Crónica* of Peter the Cruel is the most important and penetrating. Ayala is the most reliable of historians up to this time.

Didactic Poetry

Didactic poetry flourished, and indeed many of the works treated under *Juglaría* and *Clerecía* poetry were didactic. The

Book of Good Love of the Archpriest of Hita and the *Rimado de palacio* of López de Ayala were didactic, or contained many didactic elements. There are several poems, however, surviving from the fourteenth century, which are almost entirely didactic.

The *Proverbios morales* of the **Rabbi Sem Tob** (also called Santob and Santo) are of this variety. The author lived in the first half of the century and dedicated his *Proverbios* to King Peter the Cruel. The metrical form was the quatrain in heptasyllables, brought about by the division of two hemistichs of the Alexandrine line of the *clerecía* verse, with rhyme ABAB rather than the clerecía AAAA. His proverbs are the quintessence of concise wisdom. They point to a philosophical, sad, and pacific acceptance of life's trials. The language is popular and many of the proverbs are from Spanish sources. There is a strength and keenness about the book, and the Rabbi had imitators like the Marqués de Santillana. This, according to Menéndez Pelayo, was Spain's first example of gnomic literature (the literature of maxims and aphorisms). The work is also called *Consejos e documentos al rey don Pedro,* and was written between 1355 and 1360.

Two other poems are worthy of mention. The *Doctrina de la discreción* of Pedro de Veragüe was written in a verse form that somewhat resembles the *zéjel*. This longish poem explains the Creed, the Ten Commandments, the Fourteen Works of Mercy, the Sacraments, the Seven Deadly Sins, etc., and gives moral advice in general. Some consider it the oldest of Spanish catechisms. Its popularity with the people carried it into the sixteenth century.

The *Revelación de un ermitaño* is in the form of the disputes so popular in the thirteenth century (see Juglaría Poetry). Written in stanzas of *arte mayor,* it deals with the dispute between the body and the soul.

HISTORY

A number of important histories appeared in the fourteenth century. The *Crónicas* of **Pero López de Ayala** have already been mentioned. **Fernán Sánchez de Valladolid** (1315-1359) wrote *Crónicas* on the reigns of Alfonso X, Sancho IV, and Ferdinand IV. Three histories have wrongly been attributed to **Juan Núñez de Villaizán. Fernán Sánchez** was a counselor of Alfonso XI, but it is not likely that he wrote the well known *Crónica de Alfonso XI*. The *Crónica* of this eleventh Alfonso is actually of unknown authorship, but whoever wrote it must have known the *Poema de Alfonso Onceno* (see Poetry). The *Crónica*, however, goes farther than the *Poema* and adds materials not found in the poem.

The *Crónica rimada*, whose longer title is *Crónica rimada de las cosas de España desde la muerte del rey don Pelayo hasta don Fernando el Magno y más particularmente de' las aventuras del Cid*, is written in a not very inspiring *juglaría* verse. As can be seen from its title, it attempts to treat a large section of the course of Spanish history.

The *Gran conquista de Ultramar*, Spain's longest history of the Crusades (1,320 chapters) is for the most part a translation or paraphrase of the *Historia Rerum in Partibus Transmarinis Gestarum* of William of Tyre. Ultramar, of course, is the Spanish equivalent of the French *Outre Mer*, or Palestine. The siege of Acre, the part played in history by Peter the Hermit and the other well known personages, the battles, and other events of the Crusades appear. The book was written in the times of Alfonso XI and it contains interesting motifs from fiction. The truly narrative elements are imbedded in those chapters that deal with the Swan Knight, Lohengrin, related, it is said, to give the genealogy of Godfrey de Bouillon. This version of the famous theme of the Swan Knight is quite unique and is not a translation like most of the historical parts of the *Gran conquista*. There are numerous interesting motifs, and the fictitious part of the book may be regarded as the first fairy tale in Spanish. Realism is present, too, for the writer was a close observer of life and of nature. Elements of the novel of chivalry are present, also, as one would expect in a tale laid in the period of the Crusades. The prose is very clear and readable.

The histories of Don Juan Manuel will be treated under his more important works (See Prose Fiction).

PROSE FICTION

Brief Narrative

Don Juan Manuel (1282-1349?) nephew of Alfonso X, wrote the most famous book of brief narratives. The *Conde Lucanor* or *Libro de Patronio* belongs to the tradition of the *exemplum* and therefore is part of didactic literature. Its author wrote it, he said, to instruct pleasantly, and he used as sources a great many oriental tales of an ethical character, refusing to include such racy and ribald stories as those found in the *Libro de los engaños*. The stories are supposedly related by Patronio, Count Lucanor's adviser, who tells each to illustrate some counsel he is giving his master. There are actually 51 stories, but the 50 headings have lead scholars to speak of the "fifty tales" of Don Juan Manuel. None of the stories is entirely original, for Don Juan Manuel adapted them from known sources. None is a mere translation, however, and to each he has given a Spanish setting and characters. Famous among the tales are the Shrew Wife and the Emperor's New Clothes, which came from eastern fiction.

Even if the author's prose style is not a model of grace and flexibility, most will agree that, unlike many of his predecessors, he made a conscious effort to write well and that he helped to mold Castilian into the noble instrument of expression it later became.

Don Juan Manuel's *Crónicas* are worthy of note. His *Crónica abreviada* is made up of abstracts and summaries of King Alfonso's *Crónica general*. To Don Juan Manuel is also attributed the longer *Crónica complida*.

This versatile writer wrote works in other fields. His *Libro de los estados* is a book of 150 chapters in which the author paints a rather complete picture of society in the fourteenth century and shows the relationship between the various classes, stating the obligations of each to the others. The frame of the book appears to be a kind of reworking of *Barlaam and Josaphat* (see Brief Fiction, Thirteenth Century), and to this extent, of course, it is novelesque. The setting, however, is Spanish. Another of Don Juan Manuel's didactic works was the *Libro del caballero et del escudero,* the purpose of which was to teach the rules of chivalry through conversation between the *escudero* (squire) and the old knight. There is very little that can be called novelesque here. A second part of the book is a storehouse of knowledge of fourteenth-century astrology, natural sciences, etc. The sources are Ramón Lull, St. Isidore, and Alfonso X.

Still another of Don Manuel's works was the *Libro de la caza,* a detailed account on falconry in its many phases (breeding, training, etc.). It gives the better hunting areas and is probably Spain's best medieval treatise on hunting. His *Tratado de armas* is a discussion of weapons and their use, as was the lost *Libro de los engeños*.

King Sancho IV caused to be written (and may have taken part in the writing of) a book called *Castigos y documentos para bien vivir*. It is a didactic work belonging to the books written as guides of conduct for princes. King Sancho had it put together for the training of his son Ferdinand IV. The sources are pious and secular, eastern and western, and the didactic expositions, line for line, far overbalance the interpolated tales, some of which are on well-known themes. In general the prose is pure and the narration well handled.

Novelesque Prose

As might be expected, novelesque prose would quite naturally fall into certain categories. The Novel of Chivalry was one of these. *Amadís de Gaula,* Spain's greatest novel of this kind, probably originated as early as the fourteenth century, but the oldest versions in existence are of the early sixteenth century and are in print. (See Sixteenth Century Novelesque Prose.)

The *Caballero Cifar,* called the first novel of chivalry, is a book of varied content. Written about 1300, it does indeed contain chivalresque elements. However, it is by no means a typical novel of chivalry, for it has elements of the picaresque, of the Byzantine novel or Milesian tale, as well as long didactic passages illustrated by a number of well-known *exempla.* Its frame story probably comes from an Arabic tale of a king who lost all—wealth, wife, children—only to find them after many trials and tribulations. Such a tale is found in the *Arabian Nights.* There are in the *Caballero Cifar,* however, parts that may be drawn from the Breton Cycle with an underwater world and a wicked fairy queen. Proverbs are sprinkled throughout the work and there is a remarkable portrait of a squire named the Ribaldo in whom some scholars see the beginnings of Sancho Panza.

The *Doncella Teodor* is an oriental novel probably translated in the fourteenth century, although it might have crossed the language barrier in the thirteenth. The full title is *Capitulo que fabla de los exemplos e castigos de Teodor, la doncella.* The oldest edition, however, is in print and belongs to the sixteenth century. The story comes from the *Arabian*

Nights. The damsel, Teodor, overcomes all her opponents in a game of wits.

The *Crónica troyana,* not to be confused with the *Historia troyana* of the thirteenth century, deals, of course, with the same events in the Trojan War. Like all material drawn from this background it goes ultimately back to Latin and Greek originals. The immediate source, however, seems to have been the French version of Benoit de Saint Maure.

The Fifteenth Century

The Fifteenth Century

LYRIC POETRY	NARRATIVE POETRY	THE THEATER	HISTORY AND TRAVEL	NARRATIVE PROSE
The Cancionero de Baena	*The Romances or Ballads*	Gómez Manrique	Don Carlos, Prince of Viana	*Brief Fiction*
The Cancionero de Stúñiga	*Satirical Narrative Verse*	Lucas Fernández	Crónicas of Juan II and of Reyes de Navarra	Libro de los gatos
Other Lyric Poets	La danza de la muerte		Alfonso Martínez de Toledo	Libro de los ejemplos por a.b.c.
Don Pedro, Condestable de Portugal	*Coplas del provincial*		Juan Rodrigo de Cuenca	Espéculo de los legos
The Marqués de Santillana	*Coplas de Mingo Revulgo*		Fernán Pérez de Guzmán	Ysopete historiado
Fernán Pérez de Guzmán	*Coplas de ¡Ay, pandera!*		Alfonso de Palencia	*Satirical Prose*
Juan de Mena			Hernando del Pulgar	Alfonso Martínez de Toledo
Antón de Montoro			*Crónica de don Alvaro de Luna*	Didactic Prose
Gómez Manrique			Crónica popular del Cid	Enrique de Villena
Jorge Manrique			*Crónica de España abreviada*	Don Alvaro de Luna
Pedro Guillén de Segovia			Libro del paso honroso	Juan de Lucena
Rodríguez de la Cámara			Travel accounts	Fray López Fernández
Juan Alvarez Gato			Ruy González de Clavijo	Alfonso de Cartagena
Hernán Mexía			Pedro Tafur	Padre Martín de Córdoba
Fray Iñigo de Mendoza				Castigos y doctrinas
Fray Ambrosio Montesinos				*The Novel*
Juan de Padilla				Historical Novel
Rodrigo Cota de Maguaque				Pedro del Corral
Garci Sánchez de Badajoz				Novel of Chivalry
				Joanot Martorell (d. 1470)
				The Sentimental Novel
				Juan Rodríguez de la Cámara
				Diego de San Pedro
				Juan de Flores

CHAPTER 5

The Fifteenth Century

Reigns of: John II (1406-1454); Henry IV (1454-1474); Isabella of Castile and Ferdinand of Aragon (1474-1504).

The fifteenth century brought many changes to Spanish life. The reigns of John II and Henry IV had been politically a period of dissension and morally a time of decadence. With the ascension of Isabella and Ferdinand there was great change: the rebellious nobles were suppressed; the danger of Portuguese invasion was ended; the Kingdom of Granada, last stronghold of the Moors, surrendered in 1492; in this same year Columbus discovered the New World and set Spain on the road to conquest and colonization there; the Spanish Inquisition came into power; the Jews were expelled, an act that had many lasting and bad effects upon the country.

Printing came to Spain in the last years of the century, and as Spain turned from Moorish culture, she turned toward the revived classical culture of the Renaissance.

LYRIC POETRY

Lyric poetry continued to flourish and there were numerous collections of lyric verse. The works of troubadour poets from the fourteenth century were often included, and indeed, Galician-Portuguese poems were still being written, although the fifteenth century marks the beginnings of Italianate forms. The *cancioneros,* therefore, show poetry in transition from the troubadour verse (Galician-Portuguese) of the Middle Ages to the Italianate poetry of the Renaissance. Some collections of verse were *cancioneros* put together by known collectors. Two of the largest and most important are the *Cancionero de Baena* and the *Cancionero de Stúñiga*.

The ***Cancionero de Baena*** of **Juan Alfonso de Baena,** Royal Secretary of John II, contains some 576 poems by 54 poets whose names are known and 35 whose names are not. He dedicated the *cancionero* to King John around 1445. All the poets included were erudite men, and even those who wrote in Galician-Portuguese must be considered polished, courtly poets who entirely disregarded the poetry of the people. Most of the *Cancionero* poets are not great, and this fact has led men to say of the *Cancionero de Baena, "muchos poetas, poca poesía."* To some the most valuable contribution of the *Cancionero* is its description of the life of the times. Juan Alfonso de Baena deserves little fame save for having made a collection of poems. Pero Ferrús, or Ferrández, the oldest of the poets, wrote poems whose themes came from the classics and from the Breton Cycle; Alfonso Alvarez de Villasandino or de Illescas is represented in the *cancionero* by more poems (and more earthy ones) than any other poet; Garci Ferrández de Jerena wrote little of value, but because of his interesting life (he ran off with a Moorish woman and forsook Christianity) he is remembered; Diego de Valencia wrote a good deal of burlesque poetry and the best erotic verse in the *Cancionero;* the Archdeacon of Toro was one of the last to write in Galician-Portuguese; Macías el Enamorado, a true Galician, and one of the oldest poets in the book, is best known for his famous and tragic legend, which was used by later poets, as well as by playwrights. *Cancionero* poets who wrote in the Italian style were the following: Francisco Imperial, was a most erudite man, steeped in the classics, a scholar who could read Latin, Italian, French, English and even Arabic. He was a fair imitator of Dante whom he helped to introduce to Spain.

Ruy Páez de Ribera was a disciple of Imperial and a poet who used much allegory; Martínez de Medina, Diego Gonzalo deserve to be listed; Pero Vélez de Guevara, one of the noble poets of the *Cancionero,* was the nephew of the Marqués de Santillana; Juan Rodríguez del Padrón or de la Cámara, is more famous for a sentimental novel (see Novel); Ferrán Manuel de Lando, an imitator of Imperial, wrote good poems in praise of the Holy Virgin and also satirical verse.

The *Cancionero de Stúñiga* was compiled at the court of Alfonso V, who had won Naples for Aragon, by Lope de Stúñiga, and hence the *cancionero* gets its name. The poems in it are more lyric than those in Baena's collection, but there were also ballads and other popular poetry. This *Cancionero* gives something of a picture of Naples under Spanish domination. The largest number of poems by a single author are those of Carvajal or Carvajales, the first known author of ballads, the first Spanish poet to write in Italian, and an imitator of Santillana. Lope de Stúñiga's *Gentil dama esquiva* is perhaps his best poem; Torrellas, or Torrella, wrote mocking verse and was antifeministic; Juan de Villalpando was the only author save Santillana who wrote sonnets in Spanish in the fifteenth century; Juan de Valladolid, or Juan Poeta, was a kind of wandering picaro-poet who was bitterly criticized in the poems of some of his contemporaries.

Other Lyric Poets

Don Pedro, Condestable de Portugal, was the first Portuguese poet to write in Spanish. He suffered exile, ruled Catalonia, was a student, bibliophile, humanist, and numismatist. He produced both verse and prose, but was at his best as a poet. His *Coplas del contempto del mundo* (1490), a didactic poem inspired by Seneca and other moralists from the ancient world, offers nothing new, but it is written on a noble plane. His *Tragedia de la insigne reina doña Isabel* (of Portugal), which queen was his own sister, contains much poetry, although it is for the most part a kind of prose biography with a psychological approach.

The **Marqués de Santillana,** Don Iñigo López de Mendoza (1398-1458), was the greatest poet of the fifteenth century. He was a man of great culture and deep learning, and his delicate taste and fine discrimination made it possible for him to see excellence in troubadour poetry of the Galician-Portuguese school and even in native poetry of the people, as well as in the new Italian forms of verse. He produced some of the best lyrics of the entire period. His *villancicos, serranillas, canciones,* and *decires* are simple, and though modeled after popular poetry, are polished and erudite, maintaining a charming simplicity. He was also subject to Italian influence and was the first to write sonnets (42 of them) in Spanish. He wrote long allegorical poems after the style of Petrarch and Dante, and was the first to comment on the development of poetry in his *Prohemio y Carta al Condestable de Portugal.* In the Italian style was his most famous single poem, *Comedi-*

eta de Ponza, written in *arte mayor,* allegorical in approach, and modeled after Dante. It deals with the capture of Alfonso V or Aragon, the Marquis' exposition of the shifts of fortune, and the dreams of the wives of the captured princes and of the king. Such allegorical poems as the *Infierno de los enamorados, Defunsión de don Enrique de Villena,* the dialogue, *Bías contra Fortuna, Doctrinal de privados,* and the *Proverbios de gloriosa y fructuosa enseñanza* all have their merits, but are little read today.

Fernán Pérez de Guzmán (1376?-1460?) was an uncle of the Marqués de Santillana who retired from court life and wrote important historical documents as well as poems (see History). A poet of some merit, he contributed to the *Cancionero de Baena.* Perhaps his best lyric poem is *Que las virtudes son buenas de invocar y malas de platicar.*

Juan de Mena (1411-1456) was a Cordovan who studied at Salamanca and traveled to Rome. He was a supporter of the royal favorite, Don Alvaro de Luna, and an official in the pay of John II. Little else is known of his life. He was the first Spaniard to translate the *Iliad* (about which he also wrote a commentary). After Santillana he ranks as the greatest poet of the century. He cultivated the Dantesque style of poetry and showed a definite aspiration to enrich the Spanish language with Latinisms, to create a poetic language for the erudite, not for the man in the streets. An innovator, he anticipated Góngora. His best-known work is the *Laberinto de Fortuna,* known also as *Las Trescientas* from the approximate number of its strophes. The *Laberinto* shows that Mena imitated Dante, Virgil, Lucan, and others. It is a long allegorical poem, which even has the general idea of the *Paradiso* of Dante. Perhaps its greatest value lies not in the poetry itself or in the symbols called into play, but in historical episodes treated with patriotic sentiments and vision.

Antón de Montoro (1404-1480?), of a Jewish convert family, lived in Cordova until a pogrom drove him to Seville. He was considered by Mena and Santillana a good poet. He had some gifts as a festive poet and wrote good satirical verse.

Gómez Manrique (1412?-1490?) may be considered one of the better poets of the fifteenth century. He was important historically, for he supported Isabella in her struggle for power, and helped to bring her and Ferdinand together. He was a nephew of the Marqués de Santillana, was a man of learning and culture, and was varied in his poetic accomplishments as well as in the early development of drama (see Drama). His poetry has been divided into three types: erotic poems, *recuestas* (questions in the Galician-Portuguese troubadour as well as in courtly style), and couplets in the French-Provençal style.

Jorge Manrique (1440?-1479) is even more famous than his uncle, Gómez. He fought for Isabella and died in battle. He wrote some 50 poems, only one of which has given him immortal fame. This is the *Coplas que fizo Jorge Manrique por la muerte de su padre,* a long and beautiful poem which allows his personal grief to develop into the collective grief of all humanity in the face of death. The *Coplas* are memorable, even if they contain nothing original, for they deal with the transitory quality of human existence and yet show the reward of the good Christian. Their tone is simple, noble, familiar, lofty, but never grandiloquent. Longfellow translates them into English in a very worthy fashion.

The fifteenth century produced many poets. **Pedro Guillén de Segovia** (1413-1474?) wrote various types of verse—moralistic, political, satirical—but his best work is probably his *Siete salmos penitenciales,* modeled after Santillana's *Proverbios.* The Inquisition had them excised from the *Cancionero General.* Menéndez Pidal considered them almost the only translation of Biblical poetry found in medieval Spanish literature. In this work there is a simplicity of expression that makes it very readable. This author also wrote a rhyming dictionary of some importance called the *Gaya de Segovia.*

Juan Alvarez Gato (1440?-1509?) wrote several kinds of verse: amorous, moralistic, political, and pious. He was a good poet, facile in rhyming, simple in expression, and often clever. Some of his pious verses are modeled on popular songs.

Fray Ambrosio Montesino (d. ca. 1512), a Franciscan and favorite of Queen Isabella, wrote devotional poetry of note and criticized the loose life of the clergy. His poetry is simple and sincere, and he was remarkable in his adaptations of the popular *villancico* and *canción* to pious poetry. Some of his poems were written to be sung to popular tunes of the day, and he even composed pious ballads. Longer poems written by him are *Tratado del Santísimo Sacramento* and *Coplas del árbol de la Cruz.*

Hernán Mexía is the author of only ten surviving poems,

and all of these are amatory and satirical. His *Coplas en que descubre los defectos de las condiciones de damas* may be his best known work.

Fray Iñigo de Mendoza was a priest and one of the favorites of Isabella. He wrote hymns, ballads, satires (especially against women), *villancicos,* and amorous poems. His longest poem was *Vita Christi,* which appeared in his *Cancionero* printed in 1482. Into it he inserted examples of the various kinds of poetry mentioned above.

Juan de Padilla (1468-1522?) was one of the best imitators of Dante. Two poems of his survive. *Retablo de la vida de Cristo,* written in simple language, which gives the life of Jesus in verse according to the Four Gospels, is best known.

Rodrigo Cota de Maguaque, (el Tío), is best known for his dispute entitled *Diálogo entre el Amor y un caballero viejo,* written in the medieval tradition of disputes. Attributed to him with no foundation are the *Coplas de Mingo Revulgo* and the *Coplas del Provincial* (see Satirical Verse).

Garci Sánchez de Badajoz (1460?-1526?) wrote *canciones, decires,* and *villancicos* and some of his poems appeared in the *Cancionero General.* His poem, *Infierno de amor,* is a collection of songs about the most amorous and erotic poets of the period, and was actually a kind of allegorical list of such poets. He went mad, was given to wild and irreverent ways, and some of his poems reflect this. Even so, he was later praised by Lope de Vega and Juan de Valdés.

Narrative Poetry: Ballads

The *romance* or ballad forms the major part of narrative poetry in Spain, and the origin of the *romance* has been the subject of endless discussion. Some think the ballads were the more memorable sections of epics that were sung after the longer epic poem died; others hold that ballads were written to commemorate some event, character, or ideal; folklorists believe that *romances* are produced by the folk, that is, by unprofessional poets of the people. While students of literature may admit this for some ballads, they insist upon erudite authorship for others. Any or all these theories can be accepted, and indeed a combination of theories may best explain how ballads were produced. The earliest mention of *romances* is in Santillana's *Prohemio y carta* (written ca. 1445). The

Marqués did not hold *romances* in high esteem and thought they were written for the common people only.

In a sense he was right, for the ballad as a poetic form has never died, and is, indeed, to this day, the most frequently used of all verse forms. There is nothing more typically Spanish than a *romance*. Perhaps the first ballads were actually songs, but later ballads to be read or recited without music became extremely popular. The same phenomenon occurs in English, for one can read and enjoy a ballad like *Barbara Allen* as well as hear it and enjoy it when sung.

Assonance is employed in the earlier Spanish ballads rather than full rhyme, and traditionally ballads are in lines of 8 syllables. Their subject matter was varied and several attempts have been made to classify them in this respect. Spanish history, with many personages real and imaginary, has contributed much to the ballad; others deal with Charlemagne (considered a Christian hero against the Moors and therefore practically a Spanish hero) or the Breton themes (Tristan and Iseult, for example); legendary materials from almost any source; incidents from the border warfare on the Moorish frontier.

Collections of ballads were assembled early, and published early, by 1550; but the great and important collections of ballads appeared in the seventeenth century.

SATIRICAL NARRATIVE VERSE

The *Danza de la muerte,* or *Danza general,* as it is sometimes called, is a Spanish version of the well-known theme of the dance of death in which all mortals take part, for all must die. Death calls members from many levels of society, lay and clerical, from emperor and pope to the lowliest monk and poorest farmer. The poem is written in stanzas of *arte mayor* in the form of dialogue (which makes it in a sense dramatic) which indicates that it might well have been presented as a kind of play. Versions appear in Latin, German, French, etc., but the Spanish rendition is one of the best. In the 79 coplas the poem presents a mighty satire on society at various levels and reveals many of the vices and the virtues of the age.

The *Coplas del Provincial* (written ca. 1465) are some 149 satirical *coplas* fiercely attacking sinful clergy and wicked

nobles at the court of Henry IV. All the *coplas* are anonymous, suppression of them was unsuccessful, and they had a
great popularity. They are true examples of the *cántiga de
escarnio* known as early as the thirteenth century. They are
rather scurrilous than poetic. Their satire is carried out by
the device of having a priest (the provincial in charge of
monasteries and convents in a district) examine and criticize
the various nuns and monks (the courtiers and ladies at King
Henry's court) under his authority. The sinners are called
by name.

The *Coplas de Mingo Revulgo* are also scurrilous poems,
political satires against the court of Henry IV. The vehicle
of the *coplas* is this: a prophet in shepherd's guise asks
Mingo Revulgo (the common people) what evils exist in the
state, and Mingo answers that the flock has lost its shepherd
(the country its king) and points out the many evils present
in the realm.

The *Coplas de ¡Ay, panadera!* are a series of satires of the
nobles who showed cowardice at the Battle of Olmedo (1445),
when the armies of John II and Don Alvaro de Luna defeated the rebel nobles. Each *copla* contains two *redondillas*
with an *estribillo* that reads *"¡Ay, panadera!"*, hence the title.

THE THEATER

Very little drama has survived from the fifteenth century.
The *Danza de la muerte* may conceivably have been dramatic;
even the *Coplas de ¡Ay, panadera!* may have been, for they
were semidramatic in form. But plays as such are limited to only
a few writers. **Gómez Manrique** wrote a play called *Represen-
tación del Nacimiento de Nuestro Señor* for the monastery
of Calabazanos, near Palencia. He depicted the birth of Our
Lord and the adoration of the shepherds in simple language
in a play that is certainly drawn from the liturgical dramas
handed down from the Middle Ages. He also wrote *Lamen-
taciones fechas para Semana Santa* and a number of *momos*
(masques) in honor of the birthdays of certain children. Another dramatist of minor note was **Lucas Fernández** (1474-
1542), who sang in the choir at Salamanca and wrote *églogas*
and farces, some played as early as 1501. Actually, his
dramatic production belongs to the early part of the sixteenth century, but since they are in tone a part of the

fifteenth they are discussed here. In 1514 was published his *Farsas y églogas al modo pastoril y castellano* and also his *Diálogo para cantar.* He belongs to the school of Encina and therefore is part medieval and part Renaissance in his approach and handling of drama.

HISTORY

The fifteenth century produced a number of important histories. Brief mention should be made, at least, of the following, although these are not the most important: **Pablo de Santamaría** (1350-1432), a Jewish convert, wrote *Las siete edades del mundo* or *Edades trobadas,* finished ca. 1404; **Alfonso Martínez de Toledo** composed a *Vida de San Isidoro* and a *Vida de San Ildefonso,* as well as *Atalaya de las crónicas* (a kind of examination of the chronicles); **Don Carlos,** Prince of Viana, half-brother of Ferdinand of Aragon (1421-1461), an erudite and peaceful prince, more given to study than to ruling, wrote a *Crónica de los reyes de Navarra,* one of the first histories to be deliberately based upon historical documents; of unidentified authorship, the *Crónica de don Juan II* is regarded by some as the work that best shows the transition between the medieval chronicle and modern history, and is divided into chapters according to the years of King John's reign; **Juan Rodrigo de Cuenca** wrote a *Sumario de los reyes de España;* other historians were **Diego de Valera, Andrés Bernáldez,** and **Alfonso Flores.**

Fernán Pérez de Guzmán (1376?-1460?), a relative of Santillana and of Pero López de Ayala, wrote a book called *Mar de historias,* which deals with actual historical characters, ancient and medieval, such as Alexander the Great and Charlemagne. But legendary personages like Tristan and King Arthur appear in it, too, and the author apparently considered them historical. The third part of this remarkable book has come to be called *Generaciones y semblanzas,* and this is the first collection of biographies written in Spanish. These are actually short biographical sketches giving the appearance and some of the important characteristics of great men and women. The biographer was impartial and did not hesitate to praise or criticize or to describe people as he saw them, even if they appeared to him in an unflattering light.

Alfonso de Palencia (1423-1492) was very important in

this period. His *Décadas* were also known as *Crónica de Enrique IV*, but only because it was translated from the Latin in which the author originally wrote it. The Latin title was *Gesta Hispaniensia ex Annalibus Suorum Dierum*. Palencia was relatively impartial and he has given us a clear and reliable picture of the period when Princess Isabella and her brother Alfonso struggled for life and power against the evil King Henry IV.

Hernando del Pulgar (1436?-1493?) was official historian of Isabella and Ferdinand. He traveled with the monarchs, wrote a valuable history called *Crónica de los señores Reyes Católicos don Fernando y doña Isabel* (covering the years 1468-1490). His *Letras*, a collection of 32 letters addressed to various persons, contain much information of historical value. His most famous work is *Claros varones de Castilla* (written ca. 1486). This is a collection of 24 character studies of nobles at the court of Henry IV where Pulgar grew up. Physical descriptions accompany character delineation.

The *Crónica de don Alvaro de Luna*, who lived from 1385? to 1453, is of unknown authorship. It covers the entire reign of John II, and shows from its content that the author was partial to Don Alvaro de Luna, for it eulogized his life.

This period produced a *Crónica popular del Cid* (1498) which was not an original work but rather a reproduction of Chapters 35-104 of *Crónica de España abreviada* of Diego de Valera. It is important because it was popular in the fifteenth, sixteenth, and even in the seventeenth centuries, and helped to keep alive the events associated with the life of the Cid. Another lesser known work was Gutierre de Gámez' (1379-1450) *Victorial*, a chronicle that deals with legendary as well as historical materials. It is valuable as a study of aspects of daily life. Lastly, of note is the *Libro del paso honroso de Suero de Quiñones*. The book relates the strange and remarkable challenge issued by Suero to a tourney. He sent out the challenge as the result of a vow he had made to a lady (whose name is not mentioned in the account), and knights came from many parts of Europe to answer his challenge. Suero held the bridge of Orbigo against all comers during July and August of 1439. Rodrigo de Lena related the account (he was an eye-witness), but the version that has survived is the abridgment of Juan de Pineda. Such a book is valuable in the revelation it makes of the customs of fifteenth-century knights.

TRAVEL ACCOUNTS

The fifteenth century was an age of exploration and travel. Columbus wrote accounts of his voyages. Men still read the accounts of the travels of Marco Polo, translated into most European tongues, and Spain contributed to travel literature, also. At least two famous works must be mentioned in this connection. **Pedro Tafur** (1410-1484?) wrote *Andanzas y viajes de Pero Tafur por diversas partes del mundo.* It is an account of his voyages and travels through Germany, Flanders, Italy, Greece, the Near East, and North Africa. His is an instructive and pleasant account of fifteenth-century travel on land and sea. The other well-known book is **Ruy González de Clavijo's** *Historia del gran Tamorlán.* In 1403 Clavijo set out from Spain as ambassador to Tamerlane, whose court was in far-off Persia. He bore gifts from Henry III of Castile. In 1406 the embassy returned, and Clavijo wrote his famous account of the journey. Included in the work were descriptions of the places he visited, of monuments he saw, and of important personages he met. His descriptions of oriental banquets, journeys, and of the lavishness of eastern courts make interesting reading even today. They must have enthralled his contemporaries.

NARRATIVE PROSE

Brief Fiction

In the fifteenth century the popularity of *exempla* or moralized tales continued, and collections of tales both for didactic and recreational purposes were assembled. Some of the many stories set down were from medieval books like the *Disciplina Clericalis,* but others seem to have been the product of the century itself. These collections of stories were important not only for the themes they preserve or inject into Spanish literature, but also for their part in the development of Spanish prose. Narrative art reaches a high level in some of them.

The *Libro de los gatos,* in the minds of some scholars, belongs to the thirteenth century, for it is actually a translation of the thirteenth-century Latin *Fabulae* of Odo of Cheriton, an English clergyman who traveled in Spain and preached there. The stories stem from Aesopic tradition, the bestiary lore of the Middle Ages, the Cycle of Renart the Fox, and from oriental collections of apologues. Satire of evils, both lay and clerical, is bitter in the long moralizations attached to the stories, and these moralizations in the Spanish are far longer than the morals written by Odo. The extant manuscript is in a fifteenth century hand, showing that as late as this, men interested themselves in fable literature. It is written in rather artful Spanish. The title of the book may refer to cats, for cats are included in some of its stories, but there is strong likelihood that the word *gatos* has another meaning.

The *Libro de los ejemplos por a.b.c.* is the work of the Archdeacon of Valderas, **Clemente Sánchez de Vercial,** noted also for a *Sacramental* which attempted to explain a great deal about the sacraments and the obligations of men to religion. In the *Libro de los ejemplos* are some 500-odd tales arranged according to the first word of the Latin maxim that precedes each story. The book may have been meant for preachers who could select stories from the alphabetized moralizations to be used in sermons. The length of some of the tales, however, and the care and skill with which some are related may be strong evidence that they were assembled for the purpose of good and entertaining reading. The sources of Sánchez' assembled tales are extremely varied. Some come from the *Disciplina Clericalis* and *Barlaam y Josaphat;* some belong to the long tradition of the lives of the saints and the early Fathers of the Church; still others are borrowed from the well-known collections of the miracles of the Blessed Virgin; many come from the literature of classical antiquity; and some tales appear to have been drawn from the legend and folklore of the Spanish people, for they appear in no other book in Spanish or in any other language. The *Libro de los ejemplos* is Spain's longest and most varied collection of medieval tales.

Ysopete Historiado, printed in 1489, is a collection of tales, fables, anecdotes, and apologues that was translated into Spanish from the German version by Steinhöwel, this a translation in its turn of a Latin collection put together in Italy. Stories from the *Disciplina Clericalis,* Aesopic fables, and ribald as well as moralistic tales from certain Italian authors appear in it. This book, since it was available in print, may have been one of the richest sources of fable literature to men of the late fifteenth and early sixteenth centuries.

Satirical Prose

The fifteenth century was an age of satire and the greatest part of such satire appeared in prose, although there was verse satire (see Satirical Narrative Verse).

Alfonso Martínez de Toledo, Archpriest of Talavera, wrote a book which he called the *Arcipreste de Talavera.* Later writers called it the *Corbacho* and *Reprobación del amor mundano.* The book follows the ancient tradition of attacking the vices of women, and to a lesser extent the evil in men. The first part is a treatise against lust; Part II is a satirical account of, and an attack against the wiles of women, and this is the most important section of the book, for it influenced later writers and helped to develop the character of the *trotaconventos* or female go-between, made famous later in the *Celestina* at the end of the century. Part III and Part IV deal with the characters of various classes of men and the influences of the stars upon their characters. The language of the *Corbacho* is at times racy and colloquial, and it may have done a good deal to prove to Spaniards that everyday language could be successful in writing. The *Archpriest of Talavera* depicts customs and aspects of daily life realistically and often with brutal frankness. Hurtado and Palencia state that Martínez de Toledo is the only writer who truly paints family life and customs, the only satiric novelist, the only user of popular prose during the reign of John II. His other works have already been mentioned.

Didactic Prose

Don Enrique de Villena (1384-1434), a failure at politics, retired in his later years to give his life up to the study of alchemy, science, letters, and to the pleasures of the table and love. A legend of sorcery soon attached itself to this man, and this legend lasted until the past century. John II ordered his books examined, and some were burned. He wrote treatises on astronomy and the evil eye, but his most famous and valuable works were the *Doze Trabajos de Hércules,* a book that recounts the twelve famous labors of the Greek hero and explains their allegorical content, and his *Arte cisoria,* on cookery. This latter is a good source of daily life in the late Middle Ages. Villena was the first to translate (though not brilliantly) Dante's *Divine Comedy* and the *Aeneid* of Virgil into Spanish.

Don Alvaro de Luna (d. 1453), favorite of John II, was Spain's most powerful noble until the king was led to withdraw his favor and sign Luna's death warrant. His best known work is *Libro de las claras e virtuosas mujeres,* divided into three parts (women of the Old Testament, women of the Greek and Roman period, and women in Christian times). He is one of the best defenders of women and of the weaknesses of the sex. He should be remembered as feministic as opposed to the strongly anti-feministic Martínez de Toledo. He also wrote some graceful poems.

Juan de Lucena (d. 1506) wrote a *Tratado de vita beata,* a kind of conversation between the Marqués de Santillana, Juan de Mena, and Alfonso de Cartagena on the path to happiness and on the several types of human mind—contemplative, active, etc. **Fray Lope de Fernández** (mid-fifteenth century) was an Augustinian friar who wrote deeply philosophical and religious work like the *Espejo del alma* and *Libro de las tribulaciones.* **Alfonso de Cartagena** (1385-1456), an exceedingly erudite man, translated and glossed a number of important works into Spanish, thereby adding to the increasing knowledge of the century. **Padre Martín de Córdoba,** whose most memorable work, *Jardín de las nobles doncellas,* was a guide in educating the Princess Isabella (later Queen Isabella), showed women how to be virtuous by providing examples of great and good women in history. Still another work written to guide and teach women was *Castigos y doctrinas que un sabio daba a sus hijas.* It is a forerunner of such later texts as Fray Luis de León's *Perfecta casada* of the next century.

THE NOVEL

The fifteenth century brought forth important additions to novel writing, and novels of several classes appeared. There were historical novels, novels of chivalry, and especially popular, sentimental novels.

Historical Novel

Pedro del Corral's *Crónica sarracina* or *Crónica del rey don Rodrigo con la destrucción de España* (ca. 1430) may be regarded as Spain's oldest historical novel. Its sources were *crónicas* and perhaps even the *Crónica troyana*. The author retells the story of King Roderick and la Cava, giving the legend the setting of later chivalry rather than of the eighth century when the events were supposed to have taken place. Even though unoriginal (it may stem directly from the *Crónica del moro Rasis*) the work of Corral had great popularity and probably influenced the ballads. Certainly it was used by Mariana for his history more than a century later, and other writers in Spain and abroad (Sir Walter Scott, for example) made use of this rendition of the famous legend.

The Novel of Chivalry

Tirant lo Blanch, written first in Catalan and later translated into Castilian as *Tirante el Blanco,* was first printed in 1490. The author, **Joanot Martorell,** dedicated it to the Prince of Portugal. The background of the book is strange, for the author says that he translated it from English into Portuguese and then into Valencian (a dialect of Catalan). Much of it is in the vein of historical novels. It has a certain realism, later recognized and lauded by Cervantes in *Don Quijote.* Spaniards could read it in their own language after 1571.

The Sentimental Novel

Spain, influenced by Italian writers, especially Boccaccio, produced several important sentimental novels, beginning in the fifteenth century. In the *novela sentimental* love is indeed treated sentimentally, there is a good deal of allegory, much high-flown language, and the general format definitely artificial.

Juan Rodríguez de la Cámara or **del Padrón** (d. ca. 1450) composed the sentimental novel known as the *Siervo libre de amor* about 1440, basing it in part upon the *Fiammetta* of Boccaccio (mid-fourteenth century) and even more on the tragic history of the death of Inés de Castro of Portugal. It contains chivalric elements and should be considered a precursor of the sentimental novel that flowered in the sixteenth and seventeenth centuries. Its descriptions of the Galician landscape are beautiful.

Juan de Flores, about whom very little is known, wrote two sentimental novels of note, probably some time in the fourteen-eighties. His *Grimalte y Gradissa* is a sad sequel to Boccaccio's already melancholy though extremely popular *Fiammetta.* Flores' novel was translated into French by Maurice Scève of Lyons. Much more popular was the Spaniard's *Historia de Grisel y Mirabella,* a fine series of pro-feminist implausibilities which pleased Spanish, French, Italian, and English readers. There were bilingual and even polyglot versions intended to be used for teaching Spanish to foreigners. It influenced Ariosto, Lope de Vega, John Fletcher, and Georges de Scudéry.

Diego de San Pedro, of the second half of the fifteenth century, published in 1492 the *Cárcel de amor,* a sad, sad allegory in which the afflicted hero, Leriano finally pines to death because his beloved Laureola will have none of him. He still defends her, and women in general, with his dying breath. There is some real analysis of feeling, there are some chivalresque elements, and the author definitely sought refinement and elegance of style. The work was extraordinarily popular: twenty-five editions in Spanish and at least twenty in foreign languages.

The Renaissance and Humanism

The Renaissance and Humanism

LYRIC POETRY	THE THEATER	HISTORY	MYSTICS AND ASCETICS	THE NOVEL	DIDACTIC WORKS
Cancioneros: Hernando del Castillo's *Cancionero general* (1511)	Juan del Encina (1469?-1529)	Gonzalo Fernández de Oviedo (1478-1557)	Juan de Avila (1500-1569)	Fernando de Rojas, The *Celestina* (1499)	Diego de Girón (d. 1590)
	Bartolomé Torres Naharro (d. 1531?)	Francisco López de Gómara (1512?-77?)	Santa Teresa de Jesús (1515-1582)	The Novel of Chivalry:	Juan de Mal Lara (1525?-1571)
Traditional Poets:	Gil Vicente (1463-1539)	Bernal Díaz del Castillo (1492?-1581)	St. John of the Cross (1542-1591)	Amadís de Gaula (1508)	Antonio de Guevara (1480-1545)
Cristóbal de Castillejo (1490?-1550)	Lucas Fernández (1474?-1542)	Hernán Cortés (1485-1547)	Fray Luis de Granada (1504-1588)	Las sergas de Esplandián (1510)	
Gregorio Silvestre (1520-1569)	Lope de Rueda (1510?-1565)	Alvaro Núñez Cabeza de Vaca (1507?-1559)			
Italianate Poets:				The Sentimental Novel:	
Juan Boscán Almogáver (d. 1542)				Cuestión de amor (1513	
Garcilaso de la Vega (1501?-1536)				Juan de Segura, Proceso de cartas (1548)	
Gutierre de Cetina (1520-1557)				Jerónimo de Contreras, Selva de aventuras (1565)	
Francisco de Figueroa (1536-1617)					
Transition Poets:					
Diego Hurtado de Mendoza (1503-1575)					

CHAPTER **6**

The Renaissance and Humanism

Reigns of: Philip the Fair (1504-1506) ; Regency for
Joanna the Mad by Ferdinand and Cardinal
Cisneros (1506-1517) ; Charles I (1517-1556) Philip
II (1556-1598); Philip III (1598-1621).

The latter part of the fifteenth and sixteenth centuries
brought the full blossom of the Renaissance to Spain. The
vigorously revived interest in pagan antiquity, in the classics,
spread from Italy to all Europe, and Spain was no exception.
By the end of the fifteenth century and in the sixteenth, zeal
for study of the classics grew enormously in Spain, which
produced numerous noted scholars. Queen Isabella herself
had been a fair Latinist, and the royal example was followed.
The universities of Spain acquired new life. Even if a truly
pagan spirit did not prevail in Spain, there was none the
less most vigorous creative activity culminating in Cervantes,
Lope, Tirso, Calderón, and a host of others.

One observes constantly that Spain's most glorious literary
age was characterized more than elsewhere by a fusion of
medieval and of Renaissance currents, an enrichment of the
old by the new.

Antonio de Nebrija or **Lebrija** (1441-1522) was one of
Spain's great humanists. He wrote a Latin grammar (1481) ,
the first to appear written in Spanish, and in 1492 he produced a Spanish grammar, the first grammar in a modern
language. Nebrija did much to establish a standard Spanish
vocabulary and to initiate language study into Spain.

The *Polyglot Bible* inspired by Cardinal Jiménez de Cisneros (1436-1517) was one of the great contributions to Renaissance scholarship. It was put together during the years 1502-14
and 1517, in six volumes. This great monument to Biblical

studies, whose title is sometimes given as *Biblia Complutensis,* was presented in Greek, Latin, Hebrew, and Syriac. Cardinal de Cisneros served his country long and well. He founded the University of Alcalá de Henares in 1508 and served with Ferdinand as regent for Joanna the Insane until the advent of Charles V.

Juan de Valdés (d. 1541) was a fertile writer and a much traveled man, especially in Italy. His most memorable work —and to students of language and literature his most important—is his *Diálogo de la lengua,* not printed until 1737, but known to the men of his own century from the time of its writing. It is a didactic treatise in dialogue (several friends speak on the subject of the values of the Spanish language) on the relative merits of Spanish as compared with Tuscan. Valdés discusses the origins and development of Spanish, its lexicography and syntax, and does so with good judgment and appeal. Over 175 proverbs appear in the *Diálogo.*

Alfonso de Valdés, Juan's brother, wrote a *Diálogo de Lactancio y un arcediano* (known also as *Diálogo en que particularmente se tratan las cosas acaecidas en Roma en el año de 1527)* , which is a strong satire against the bad morality of churchmen; his *Diálogo de Mercurio y Carón* (1528) deals with contemporary historical events. Alfonso de Valdés, unlike his brother, actually left the Church.

Collections of proverbs, always considered a part of didactic writing, continued to be made, both in the fifteenth and in the sixteenth century. The Marqués de Santillana in the fifteenth century saw the value of such sayings, and in the sixteenth men like Pedro Valles (*Libro de refranes,* 1549) and Sebastián de Horozco (*Refranes glosados,* 1550).

Historically the sixteenth century was an important time for Spain and her people. Ferdinand and Isabella's important reign had seen the discovery of the New World and the centralization of government, as well as the expulsion of the Moors and the Jews. The Holy Inquisition had been set in motion. The marriage of Isabella's daughter Joanna (called la Loca, due to her madness) to Philip of the House of Hapsburg, gave to Spain through the offspring of Philip and Joanna a new ruling family in the person of Charles I of Spain (who was Charles V of the Holy Roman Empire) . During his reign the Moriscos were finally made to submit;

the rebel nobles and communes were overcome; the conquistadores won for Spain the great Indian empires (Aztec, Maya, and Inca) and took from lesser Indian peoples great areas of land. Philip II made Madrid the national capital, fought the religious wars, attacked England with the Spanish Armada (1588), which stands as Spain's symbolic failure.

LYRIC POETRY

This was a period of transition from native poetic manners to lyric styles brought in from Italy. Poets like Castillejo struggled to preserve the older poetic manners, while others like Garcilaso and Boscán preferred Italianate verse forms. The greater poets of the period tended to follow their lead, but combining traditional measures with the newer importations. Poetry was held in high esteem, and various manners developed. The tendency was to forsake relative simplicity and to seek greater complications and ornateness.

Traditional Poets
Cristóbal de Castillejo (1490?-1550) was a well-known priest and teacher as well as a lyric poet. His amorous compositions (*Un sueño*), *coplas* directed to a number of ladies, and a number of *obras de pasatiempos* in the vein of the medieval *cántigas de escarnio* should not be forgotten. He wrote also a *Diálogo entre el autor y su pluma;* devotional works like *Diálogo y discurso de la vida de corte;* and an attack upon those who used Italianate meters, *Contra los que dejan los metros castellanos y siguen los italianos* (written about 1540).

Gregorio Silvestre (1520-1569) was also a traditional poet. Although born in Lisbon, he made his literary reputation in Spain, writing in Spanish. He composed songs, *entremeses,* glosses of old poems, and preferred the old Castilian style to the new Italianate even when writing on classical themes like his *Fábula de Dafne y Apolo.*

Italianate Poets
The noble **Juan Boscán Almogáver** (d. 1542) studied under the humanist Lucio Marineo Sículo, and was attached to the household of Ferdinand and Isabella. He was trained in the Castilian manner of writing verse, but as the result of a

meeting with the Italian ambassador, Andrea Navagero, he took an interest in Italianate meters and he is considered the first Spaniard to naturalize Italian verse in the Spanish language. He popularized the use of *octava rima,* using Italian hendecasyllables (ABABABCC), helped to establish the use of blank verse (*verso suelto*) which he may even have introduced. He wrote some 92 sonnets in Spanish and popularized this form of poetry which had been introduced earlier by Santillana. Boscán's sonnets were written in imitation of Petrarch's. His translation of Castiglione's the *Cortegiano* (1534) rates as one of the best examples of Spanish prose in the century. He was a friend of Garcilaso de la Vega, who encouraged him in the use of Italianate verse forms. Boscán's importance lies in his innovations rather than in the quality of his poetry.

Garcilaso de la Vega (1501?-1536) was a man of noble birth and bearing and the "ideal knight" of the sixteenth century—handsome, cultured, a fine musician, poet, steadfast lover, and a member of the royal household. He campaigned with Charles V in Italy, was banished to Naples, where he met Italian verse and fell in love with it. He was wounded mortally while still young in a battle in France.

Garcilaso's poetic production was small, but its quality was excellent in the extreme. He wrote 1 epistle, 2 elegies, 3 eclogues, 5 *canciones,* 38 sonnets, 3 Latin odes, and some minor poems. Love was his principal theme, and his love poems are perfect and in no way labored as were Boscán's. Garcilaso established firmly the use of the sonnet in Spanish. His poetry is characterized as being emotional, beautiful, measured, harmonious. Many regard his first eclogue, *Salicio y Nemoroso* as his masterpiece. It was written in stanzas of fourteen lines of eleven and seven syllables and it relates the sad love affair of the shepherds, perhaps both representing the author himself, Salicio, and Nemoroso. The influence of Garcilaso upon contemporary poets was great and his poems were cited by great poets like Herrera. His language, always the purest Castilian, was delicate, simple, and extremely harmonious. He was truly a great poet. Even today, at a time when the pastoral convention is out of date, he is charming to lovers of good poetry.

Gutierre de Cetina (1507-1557?) was a noble poet who followed the styles of Italian verse and drew inspiration from such classical poets as Ovid, Juvenal, and Martial. He wrote some 244 sonnets, some of which are the equal of any written in Spanish. His *canciones,* also in the Italian style, as well as his madrigals, are delicate, light, and graceful. Perhaps his most famous poetic production is the madrigal *"Ojos claros, serenos. . . ."*

Francisco de Figueroa (1536-1617?) studied while a young man in Italy and learned to write *canciones* and other poems after the Italian way. In his old age he turned to other things and ordered his works burned, but some were saved. He was dubbed by his contemporaries as *"el divino"* and one of his famous sonnets was *A los ojos de Fili.* The influence of Horace and of the pastoral theme influenced him, as did the poems of Garcilaso.

Francisco Sá de Miranda (1485-1558) was the first Portuguese poet to write Italianate verse in Portuguese. He also wrote 75 compositions in Spanish, among which were pastorals, elegies, and sonnets. He was the first to adapt the royal octave to Portuguese.

Transition Poets

Diego Hurtado de Mendoza (1503-1575) was a true humanist, a student of Latin, Hebew, Greek, and Arabic. He attended the Council of Trent and was ambassador in several countries. He felt the influence of Italian meters, but he followed also traditional Castilian verse forms and hence is regarded as a poet of transition. His poetry in Italian meters is inferior to his work in Castilian verse forms, and he excelled especially in the native *redondilla.*

THE THEATER

The late fifteenth and early sixteenth century saw continuations of native dramatic development in the tradition of Encina's *Eglogas* as well as of Italian techniques.

Juan del Encina (1469?-1529) is the most noteworthy playwright of the fifteenth century and should be considered the first we know as a dramatist. His plays are known as *églogas* and they were not presented in public, but rather in the privacy of the palace of the Dukes of Alba, before Prince John and before Cardinal Arborea in Rome. Encina has made into secular plays the medieval mystery plays and farcical *juegos* *de escarnio* mentioned in the *Siete Partidas of Alfonso X,* but not preserved. Encina's drama is characterized by simpleness of line and setting and by the colloquial language of the players, who speak a rustic dialect. Encina produced some really humorous dialogue in the *Auto del repelón,* a conversation between two peasants who clash with students from Salamanca. There is also a good deal of vulgarity and coarseness in their speech, all of which added to the humor. The *Egloga de Plácida y Vitoriano* is perhaps Encina's most ambitious drama and it shows markedly the influence of Italian works. So also is the *Egloga de Fileno.*

In addition to his fame as a dramatist Encina is known, though here his reputation is not so great, in the field of lyric poetry. His interest in poetry was united to some skill and excellence in music, so that his poems were sometimes really songs. The majority of his poetic works were published in 1496 in his *Cancionero,* which contains also a kind of study of poetry, *Arte de la poesía castellana.* His poems were religious, erotic, burlesque, patriotic. His pastoral *villancicos* are considered among the best of such poetry in Spanish.

Encina translated Virgil's *Eclogues* and *Bucolics* and drew upon the works of other classical authors. Even so, he is usually thought of as closer to the Middle Ages than to the Renaissance.

Bartolomé de Torres Naharro (d. 1531?) brought new ideas into Spanish drama. He had been to Italy and he was able to inject new plots, theatrical arguments, and spectacle into the drama of Spain. His *Propaladia (First Fruits of Pallas)* which was published in 1517, contained not only plays, but the first set of dramatic rules in Spanish. The author stated that plays should have five acts, not less than 6 nor more than 12 characters, and that there were two types of plays: *comedia a noticia* (realistic plays dealing with customs) and *comedia a fantasia* (imaginary plays dealing particularly with intrigue). His *Comedia tinelaria* and *Comedia soldadesca* are *comedias a noticia,* since both are plays of manners or customs; more famous is his *Comedia Himenea,* the most celebrated and successfully contrived play of the early Spanish theater.

Gil Vicente (1465-1539) was a Portuguese actor, director, and playwright who borrowed ideas from the *Celestina* and from Torres Naharro and Juan del Encina, as well as themes from well-known ballads and certain of the novels of chivalry. Eleven of his plays are in Spanish, twelve are in Portuguese, and the rest are a mixture of these languages. His *Don Duardos* and *Amadis de Gaula* are the first plays in Spanish based upon chivalric themes. His dramatic style was not of the best but he is famous for his characters, which excel those of Encina. His *Comedia del viudo* (1514) contains fine humor and in the minds of some critics is his best dramatic production.

Lope de Rueda (1510?-1565) wrote pastoral plays that were an improvement over all previous plays of this sort in Spanish. He was a most versatile man, for he was a theater manager, impresario, actor, as well as a dramatist. He is particularly famous for his *pasos* (short, one-act plays based upon manners and customs of the people). Such *pasos* were often presented just before Act I of a long play, or at some convenient place in the middle of it. The *pasos* of Lope de Rueda had little action, their characters were commoners, but they were very skillfully done. His plays, like others in the period before the construction of theaters, were presented in the plazas of the towns or in *corrales* (streets closed off to form temporary theaters). *Las aceitunas* is an excellent one-act play, and some have even considered it the best one-act play written in Spanish. Plays drawn from the manners of the common people, then, give Lope de Rueda a place of fame, for his Plautian dramas offer nothing original and his Italianesque plays fall into the same pattern. Rueda had less successful imitators.

HISTORY

The Renaissance was a period of history, for the exploration, conquest, and colonization of the New World afforded much material.

Gonzálo Fernández de Oviedo (1478-1557), a conquistador, wrote a *Historia general y natural de las Indias* (first printed in 1535, Part I). It is a valuable work, containing in addition to actual history and events some unique and very remarkable accounts of natural history, mineral, botanical, and zoological.

Francisco López de Gómara (1512?-1557?) was one of Cortés' captains and his great admirer. His histories tell of the discovery of the New World by Columbus and recount the conquest of Mexico.

Bernal Díaz del Castillo (1492?-1581) wrote one of the most interesting and realistic of all histories, his *Verdadera historia de la conquista de la Nueva España*. It is a long and detailed work and shows the soldier's viewpoint rather than the officer's. Bernal Díaz is impartial, straightforward, and simple in his approach to the conquest of the Aztecs by Cortés, and he held back little. He set down what he saw and gave a good account of native customs as well as with the events of the conquest.

Hernán Cortés (1485-1547), who led the incredible expedition that overcame the mighty empire of Montezuma, wrote an account of his actions in the form of letters addressed to King Charles V. He gave in simple and direct language his conception of the importance of the conquest of Mexico, reported the customs and habits, and of course, the wealth of the Aztecs, and the importance of his own and his men's part in the struggle. The letters are considered admirable as models of epistolary history.

Alvaro Núñez Cabeza de Vaca (1507?-1559) who explored vast areas of what is now the United States (the Gulf States) in 1542 wrote *Naufragios,* a vivid and moving account of his wanderings. He describes the plains Indians, the herds of buffalo, and paints a realistic picture of the land and the times.

MYSTICS AND ASCETICS

Spanish mysticism holds an important place in Spanish life and in the history of Spanish literature. The great period of the mystics, almost the entire sixteenth century, produced a very characteristic manifestation of the religious genius of Spain, making itself felt in both clerical and lay circles. Mysticism, no new thing, had existed in the ancient world, the Orient, in the Middle Ages. It reached new heights in Spain, however, in the sixteenth century. Ramón Lull had been a great mystic in the fourteenth century; Spanish Arabs and Jews (Averroes and Avempace) had been; León Hebreo (1460?-1520) in his *Dialogues of Love* had written much that the later mystics read and drew upon, and this work had been translated into Spanish from Italian as early as 1568.

There was, then, a tradition for mysticism for Spaniards to follow. The Spanish mystics sought to approach God not through syllogistic reasoning but through constant meditation, until the soul achieved oneness with its Maker. The book in the Bible which most inspired the mystics was the *Song of Solomon.*

Juan de Avila (1500-1569) was a great preacher in Andalusia, celebrated for his oratorical gifts and for his sanctity. His writings influenced others, such as Fray Luis de Granada. He exchanged letters with Santa Teresa.

Santa Teresa de Jesús, whose secular name was Teresa Sánchez de Cepeda y Ahumada (1515-1582), was one of the most remarkable women of her time. Hers was an active life, for she founded convents and did much to reform the Carmelite Order. She carried on correspondence with many important people, and among her works she gives us a good account of her early life in her native Avila (*Libro de su vida,* and *Libro de las fundaciones.* Her mystic works, however, are her claim to literary greatness: *Camino de perfección* (1583); *Conceptos del amor de Dios . . .* (1612); and above all her *El castillo interior o las moradas* (written 1577, printed 1583) in which she shows the ascent of her soul through the seven chambers of the mystic castle to the bosom of God. Her works were mainly in prose, but she wrote fine poems for her nuns. She is often called *la Doctora Mística.*

San Juan de la Cruz (St. John of the Cross, 1524-1591) was born plain Juan de Yepes y Cepeda, near Avila, and was a fellow-townsman and fellow-Carmelite with St. Teresa, twenty-six years older, who influenced him. He professed in 1564, and rose to important positions in the Reformed Carmelite Order. Like St. Teresa and other mystics, he was extremely active externally, although his spirit was given over to profound religious meditations.

His works were not published (1618) until after his death. They were called *Obras espirituales,* and are fundamentally three prose meditations on poems, the *Subida del Monte Carmelo, Noche oscura del alma,* and *Llama de amor viva.* The graceful poetic form is the *lira,* so happily used by Garcilaso and Fray Luis de León. The general theme is the union of the soul with God; the human symbol, inspired by the *Song of Solomon,* is the union of lover and beloved. The mystic aspiration has never been more beautifully expressed in verse, and one does not have to subscribe to any particular theology to enjoy the sheer loveliness of the poetry, in which the mystic ideal reaches supreme expression. St. John is at the top of the more than three thousand mystic and ascetic writers whom Spain is said to have produced.

A sonnet of uncertain date and authorship is deserving of mention, the *Soneto a Cristo Crucificado*. It is a beautiful expression of what has been termed "divine intoxication."

Fray Luis de Granada, whose secular name was Luis Sarria (1504-1588), brought the works of such men as Cicero and St. Augustine to the uneducated in Spain in a flowing style admired by many. He also translated Thomas à Kempis. In his own time he was best known as a preacher and moralist, and his famous *Guía de pecadores,* which reveals the path to virtue, was extremely popular. Another religious work was his *Símbolo de la Fe* (1582) which shows the rise of man from his earthy state to an understanding of the Roman Catholic faith.

Other mystic writers have left their names, but none are so famous as St. Teresa, St. John of the Cross, and Fray Luis de León (see Lyric Poetry). **Fray Malón de Chaide** wrote *Libro de la conversión de la Magdalena* in 1588, a work that contains, aside from the moralistic and erudite treatment of this subject, some informative translations and paraphrases of certain of the Psalms. This book was one of the most esteemed of its time. **Fray Juan de los Angeles** wrote *Triunfos del amor de Dios* in 1590; **Alonso de Orozco** (1500-1591) wrote *Historia de la Reina Sabá* (1565); and **Diego de Estella** (1524-1578) his *Tratado de la vida de San Juan.*

THE NOVEL

Fernando de Rojas and the *Celestina*

In 1499 there appeared in Burgos a sixteen-act *Comedia de Calisto y Melibea,* reprinted in other cities in 1500 and 1501. In 1502, in Seville it appeared in twenty-one acts, and the title was *Tragicomedia de Calisto y Melibea.* Acrostic verses tell us that the author was Fernando de Rojas. This Rojas, whose biography is unhappily obscure, was of Jewish origins, a lawyer who became chief magistrate of the town of Talavera near Toledo. Just when he was born and died is not known.

The dates 1475?-1537? have been suggested. In his great work, a "letter from the author to a friend of his" states that he originally found the first (and by far the longest) act, and in *"quince días de vacaciones"* added the other fifteen. In the edition of 1502 the implication is that the same Rojas inserted the five new acts between the former Acts XIV and XIX. The question of authorship has been long debated. The great scholar Menéndez Pidal thinks that the first act is by a different author, but that Rojas added all the twenty following acts, possibly with a collaborator. Many scholars are now willing to agree with that opinion.

All problems aside, we are fortunate in possessing this work of genius, which was early called by the name of the dominant character, *La Celestina.* She and all the other characters involved present themselves and their vital attitudes solely by means of dialogue, an important feature of the author's technique. The plot is simple in outline, even simpler than that of *Romeo and Juliet,* with which it has important parallels. The young and gallant Calisto comes upon the even nobler and very lovely maiden Melibea in her garden. Infinitely enamored, desperate, impatient to win her, he has recourse to a gifted and skillful old hag, Celestina, who reminds us of the *trotaconventos* of the *Book of Good Love* and of the *Corbacho.* She most efficiently overcomes Melibea's maidenly scruples, and Calisto is given an appointment in her chamber. Celestina, as selfish as she is crafty, quarrels with her two accomplices, who are Calisto's servants, over the division of the reward she has received, and they kill her. They themselves are swiftly caught and executed. Calisto, climbing down a ladder from Melibea's room, misses his footing and falls to his death in the street below. For Melibea life has no substance without Calisto. She summons her aging father, explains to him what has happened, and hurls herself from a high tower. The book ends with the father's poignant lament: his personal grief, his protest against a world ruled by disorder and the cruel might of a blind Eros.

Why have competent critics rated the *Celestina* just after the *Quixote* as the second greatest production of Spanish literary genius? One may suggest that it is an impressive confrontation of two aspects of life, the lofty and the low, the idealistic and the realistic, even the ethereal and the earthy.

The passion of the high-born Calisto and Melibea, sensual in essence, is far-removed from any thoughts of material advantage, even of social propriety. It is an intense love which exists in and for itself, quite outside conventionality. The final result, brought about through the unhappy accident due to Calisto's carelessness, was tragedy. Just how seriously are we to take the author's statement that his work was written "in reproof of mad lovers, who adore their beloved ones and call them their God, and in reproof of untrustworthy procuresses and false retainers?" The work turns out to be far richer than any mere homily.

The author, steeped in both medieval and Renaissance thought, sees and presents two worlds, the aristocratic milieu of Calisto and Melibea and her parents, and the baser world presided over by "the old witch of a whore," Celestina. The lovers are incapable of base thoughts, of any desire for material advantage and are wholly devoted to their overwhelming love for each other. Celestina and her cohorts are incapable of noble love, but they have a great deal of practical sense. Celestina, observant and experienced, knows how to turn the passions of others to her own advantage. She explains that, as a procuress she does not seek out others, they come to her, and she is merely trying to support herself. Her greed and the violence of Calisto's servants cause the death of all three.

Rojas presents the two separate worlds, the idealistic and the basely realistic, not separately but together, in contact, with their effects upon one another. The realistic elements point the way to an aspect of the picaresque novel, the idealistic to the courtly novel of the future, and both to the Spanish *comedia,* to the marvelous duality of *Don Quixote.*

The great characterization is, of course, Celestina herself, but all the characters, high and low, are carefully distinguished and artistically delineated.

The speech of aristocrats and proletarians is also highly appropriate. The former speak in phrases which betoken their early Renaissance education with many classical references, often in rather high-flown rhetoric. The backstreet characters possess a racy and colloquial speech which entirely befits them, and which is perhaps a little less harsh and rough than readers are likely to encounter in certain modern novels. The style is picturesque without pruriency. The contemporary humanist Juan de Valdés said of the work: "No book has ever been written in Castilian in which the language is more natural, fitting, and elegant."

The *Celestina* was the first Spanish book to be translated into English. Three English translations have very recently appeared in America, and it was relatively early translated into most European languages.

The Novel of Chivalry

Amadís de Gaula was first printed in 1508, although it had been known in the Peninsula for perhaps two centuries. Apparently Garci Rodríguez de Montalvo took the ancient text, which he called *"Antiguos originales,"* corrected and enlarged it (this concerns the first three books), and then wrote a fourth book. *Amadís de Gaula* stemmed in general from Arthurian legends. Its period of great popularity came with Montalvo's version, and it was to attain to the distinction of being the most widely read and important of all the books of chivalry. The romantic origin of Amadís, the book's vague geography, the chivalric love affair of the hero and his beloved, the Lady Oriana, the dauntless courage and incredible hardihood and strength of Amadís, and his purity of heart made of *Amadís de Gaula* a kind of "blue book" of courtly manners and morals. Amadís was the perfect knight and lover. This book set the pattern for subsequent novels of chivalry. All classes of society knew *Amadís*.

Las sergas de Esplandián, published in 1510, was a sequel to *Amadís de Gaula* and was also the work of Montalvo. It related the *sergas* (deeds) of Esplandián, son of Amadís and Oriana, and it thrilled its readers in the sixteenth century even though modern readers may feel that there is a certain sameness in all the adventures. The *Amadís* Cycle finally grew to 23 books.

Other cycles grew up, and there were numerous independent productions. The Books of Chivalry could offer readers a lifetime of amusement and they were enormously popular throughout the whole sixteenth century. Long before 1600 their popularity had begun to wane and the time was ripe for a satirical treatment of them. Cervantes proved that point in 1605.

The Sentimental Novel

The vogue of the sentimental novel continued after the times of Diego de San Pedro and Juan de Flores (see Sentimental Novel in 15th century).

The *Cuestión de amor,* (1513) is a sentimental novel with psychological overtones. It is a *"novela de clave,"* and some of the characters have been identified. It is a picture of court life in Naples in which real names of people are half-disguised by pseudonyms. Written partly in prose and partly in verse, this work is most valuable to us as a picture of daily life with all the color and lavish spectacle of the sixteenth century.

Juan de Segura's sentimental work, *Proceso de cartas de amores que entre dos amantes pasaron* (1548) has been declared the first full-fledged epistolary novel in Europe. The style is elevated and the story sentimentally sad.

Jerónimo de Contreras' *Selva de aventuras* gained great popularity in its day. More original than some works in this period, it related the adventures of two lovers who turned to the cloistered life. It was published in 1565.

DIDACTIC WORKS

Diego Girón (d. 1590) was a noted humanist who translated the *Fables of Æsop.* His Castilian poems were in imitation of Virgil, Seneca, and Valerius Flaccus, and his rendition of Horace's *Beatus Ille* is still admired.

Juan de Mal Lara, (1525?-1571), the important Sevillian humanist, also collected proverbs and wove tales around them in a strange book called *Philosophia vulgar* (1568). The book was modeled upon the *Adagia* of Erasmus, whose influence was strong in Spain. We must regard Mal Lara as an early Spanish folklorist, as well as humanist.

Antonio de Guevara (1480-1545) was one of the most popular writers of the sixteenth century. He was a Franciscan and even became a bishop. His *Reloj de príncipes con el Libro de Marco Aurelio* (published 1529) is a combination of two books. Almost entirely fictitious, it is based upon the life of Marcus Aurelius and it attempts to show how this Roman emperor was the perfect Christian prince. It influenced foreign writers and it was translated and esteemed in France and England. Guevara's *Menosprecio de corte y alabanza de* *aldea* (1539) praises rural simplicity versus urban complexities. The *Décadas* (1539) are well known, being a set of ten biographies of Roman emperors. Guevara's elegance can still be savored in those works and in his letters.

The Golden Age

The Golden Age

LYRIC POETRY	THE DRAMA	HISTORY	MISCELLANEOUS PROSE
The Northern School:	Juan de la Cueva (1543-1610)	Jerónimo Zurita (1512-1580)	Didactic Literature:
Fray Luis de León (1527-1591)	Andrés Rey de Artieda (1549-1613)	Ambrosio de Morales (1513-1591)	Francisco Gómez de Quevedo (1580-1645)
Pedro Malón de Chaide (1530?-1589)	Lope Félix de Vega Carpio (1562-1635)	Florián de Ocampo (1495?-1558)	Diego de Saavedra Fajardo (1584-1648)
Benito Arias Montano (1527-1598)	Gabriel Téllez, Tirso de Molina (1584?-1648)	New World Histories:	Sebastián de Covarrubias y Orozco (d. 1613)
Francisco Sánchez (1523-1600)	Ruiz de Alarcón (1581?-1639)	Padre Bartolomé de las Casas (1474-1566)	
Francisco de la Torre (mid-sixteenth century)	Antonio Mira de Amescua (1574?-1644)	Garcilaso de la Vega, el Inca (1540-1615)	
Francisco Medrano (last half of sixteenth century)	Luis Vélez de Guevara (1579-1644)	Spanish History:	
The Southern School:	Luis Quiñones de Benavente (d. 1652)	Padre Juan de Mariana (1535?-1624)	
Fernando de Herrera (1534-1597)	Juan Pérez de Montalbán (1602-1638)		
Luis de Góngora y Argote (1561-1627)	Francisco de Rojas Zorrilla (1607-1648)		
Baltasar del Alcázar (1530-1606)	Guillén de Castro (1569-1631)		
Juan de Arguijo (1567-1623)	Agustín Moreto (1618-1669)		
Juan de Jáuregui (1583-1641)	Pedro Calderón de la Barca (1600-1681)		
Rodrigo Caro (1573-1647)			
Francisco de Rioja (1583-1688)			
Esteban Manuel de Villegas (1589-1658)			
The Prince of Esquilache (1577-1658)			
Lupercio L. de Argensola (1559-1613)			
Bartolomé L. de Argensola (1562-1631)			

The Golden Age

LYRIC POETRY	NARRATIVE POETRY	THE NOVEL	CERVANTES
Pedro Espinosa (1578-1650)	Alonso Hernández	The Pastoral Novel:	*La Galatea* (1585)
Juan de Tassis y Peralta (1582-1622)	Luis Zapata (1526-1595)	Jorge de Montemayor (1520?-1561)	*Don Quijote,* Part I (1605) Part II (1615)
Salvador Jacinto Polo de Medina (1603-1676)	Luis Barahona de Soto (1548-1595)	Gaspar Gil Polo (d. 1591)	*Novelas ejemplares* (1613)
Francisco Trillo de Figueroa (d. ca. 1660)	Juan Rufo (1547?-1620)	Luis Gálvez de Montalvo (1546?-1591?)	*Viaje del Parnaso* (1614)
Alonso Ledesma (1562-1623)	Cristóbal de Virués	The Moorish Novel:	*Ocho comedias y ocho entremeses* (1615)
Francisco Gómez de Quevedo (1580-1645)	Alonso de Ercilla y Zúñiga (1533-1594)	The *Abencerraje*	Byzantine Novel:
Fray Hortensio Félix Paravicino (1580-1633)	Pedro de Oña (1570?-1643)	The Picaresque Novel:	*Los trabajos de Persiles y Sigismunda* (1617)
Sor Juana Inés de la Cruz (1651-1695)	Ballads	Francisco Delicado	
		Lazarillo de Tormes (1554)	
		Mateo Alemán (1547-1614?)	
		Francisco López de Ubeda (d. 1596)	
		Francisco de Quevedo (1580-1644)	
		Luis Vélez de Guevara (1579-1644)	
		Alonso Jerónimo de Salas Barbadillo (1580-1635)	
		Alonso de Castillo Solórzano (1584-ca. 1648)	

CHAPTER 7

The Golden Age

Reigns of: Philip III (1598-1621); Philip IV (1621-1665); Charles II (1665-1700).

The fruitful inspiration of the Italian Renaissance had beneficially affected Spanish genius from the late fifteenth century onward, yet Spain has never blindly accepted anything from outside. The process has regularly been *La españolización de lo de fuera* (the Hispanizing of everything from outside). The gorgeous efflorescence of literary and other arts in Spain's Golden Age came when Spanish genius absorbed and assimilated elements from abroad, notably from Italy.

The process may be readily observed in lyric poetry. Boscán and Garcilaso wrote enthusiastically and almost exclusively in the new Italian manner, forsaking traditional Spanish patterns. Their successors achieved a fusion of the old and the new. In considering Spain, the observer is always impressed with the utilization throughout the Renaissance of medieval elements. One can see it in lyric poetry, in the *Quixote,* in the Spanish *comedia,* everywhere.

The literary art in Spain in the early Renaissance was in general simple in style. As the age progressed there was a tendency toward greater ornamentation and complication, toward what is broadly called the baroque. Its chief manifestations in Spain are called conceptism and Gongorism, which will be considered in connection with appropriate authors.

LYRIC POETRY

It is convenient although not entirely accurate to speak of two schools of poetry in Spain after the mid-sixteenth century, the northern and the southern, of the School of

Salamanca and the School of Seville. It is to be understood that poets from all parts of Spain exhibited the characteristics of both in varying degrees. The Salamancans emphasized content over manner and sought classical purity, sobriety within the realm of lyric intensity.

The Northern School (Salamanca)

Fray Luis de León (1527-1591) is the most famous representative of this school. Fray Luis, of Jewish origins, studied to become an Augustinian monk and took his vows at the age of seventeen. He studied under great teachers and became a noted teacher himself at the University of Salamanca, where he held chairs of theology. He was accused of championing the Hebrew text of Holy Scripture in preference to the Vulgate and was put in prison (1572-1576) by the Inquisition. He wrote a greater volume in prose than in verse (translations, theological works, *Los nombres de Cristo,* and *La perfecta casada*), but his chief fame rests upon his poetry and he is considered by many the greatest of all Spanish lyric poets of all time. Some of his poems are beautiful and clear poetic translations of Biblical poetry (the First Psalm translated into *liras*), translations from classical poets, notably from Horace, whose poems Fray Luis most delicately renders in Spanish. He has even been called the "Christian Horace." Luis de León achieves a true fusion of Hebraic-Christian and classical-pagan elements. His best poems are written in *liras,* the form naturalized by Garcilaso. Noteworthy are *A Francisco Salinas* (on music), *Noche serena* (the inspiration for transforming the terrestrial into the celestial), *A Felipe Ruiz* (man's longing for heavenly beauty and perfect knowledge), and the *Vida retirada* (plain and satisfying existence away from the hurly-burly of life). Luis de León's poetry is simple though perfect in expression, lofty in thought and inspiration. There are good reasons for considering him Spain's foremost lyric poet.

Other poets, from various parts of Spain, displayed Horatian influences and cultivated simplicity rather than elaborateness, following along general lines the manner of Luis de León. Among them may be mentioned: **Pedro Malón de Chaide** (1530?-1589), **Benito Arias Montano** (1527-1598), **Francisco Sánchez "El Brocense"** (1523-1600), **Francisco de la Torre,**

about whom little is known except for his delicate verse, and
Francisco de Medrano (1570-1607).

The Southern School of Poets (Seville, Cordova)

A tendency toward the emphatic and ornate style is observable in the verse of Herrera, and the progression toward
baroque art was steady. The remark is true in all Europe,
showing itself as euphuism in England, marinism in Italy,
preciosity in France, and Schwulst in Germany. In Spain it is
considered under two heads: conceptism and Gongorism.
Those who oppose any sort of elaborateness in art do well
to remember that later Renaissance artists were seeking enrichment and not exaggeration, improvement over a commonplace manner of expression. The plane surface was likely to
be covered with decoration, the straight line to be broken or
curved, or even scrolled.

Theoretically conceptism applied to thought, and the
"concepto" was meant to be a striking metaphor, and original
conceit, even a striking play on words, a stimulating mental
quirk. All sorts of figures of speech were utilized by the
conceptistas: antithesis, parallelism, oxymoron (the combining of impossible opposites like "warm ice," "living corpse"),
chiasmus (inversion of the second member of two parallel
statements). All readily admit that poetry is enriched by
metaphors, but those of the conceptists were likely to become
strained, and their excessive use a mannerism. A genius like
Quevedo, in both prose and verse, could achieve admirable
effects, but less gifted imitators were likely to go astray, and
did.

The *cultos, culteranos,* or Gongorists, as they are called,
tried to enrich their works with strange and beautiful words,
many borrowed from Latin, with all sorts of historical and
mythological allusions, even with a Latinized syntax, with
elaborate and ornate comparisons, including metaphors. They
achieve effects of rare beauty, but their poetry was likely to
be only for the initiated, for the highly cultured like themselves. There is probably no point in trying to distinguish
sharply between conceptism and *culteranismo,* because they
are parallel and most cultured authors displayed both tendencies. One sees evidences even in the works of authors who
considered themselves free from every taint of affectation. It
may be remarked that the *cultistas* enriched the Spanish

vocabulary with many new words which were then considered strange neologisms and are today accepted as completely normal and usual.

The Southern School (Seville)

Fernando de Herrera (1534-1597) was a secular priest of humble birth and one of several poets to hold the soubriquet of "*el divino.*" The acknowledged early leader of the Southern School of poets, he is characterized by brilliant and rich imagination. He wanted to employ more noble and lofty themes in poetry and do so in specifically poetic dress. To accomplish this he studied the Greek and Roman poets, as well as the Bible; he replaced native words and expressions with others modeled upon Greek and Latin; his poems were filled with archaisms and even neologisms, and metaphor and inversion were frequent devices with him. He even invented a novel system of spelling. Herrera went so far as to set down some of his reforms in his annotated edition of Garcilaso's poetry (1580).

Herrera's love poetry is fairly conventional, but he is considered one of Spain's greatest patriotic poets, and his patriotic poetry is sweeping, powerful, and inspiring. His *Canción a la victoria de Lepanto* (1572) is a noteworthy example, and line succeeds line with a mighty roll. This poem, with the ode *Por la pérdida del Rey Don Sebastián,* is numbered among the *Canciones* upon which his greatest fame rests.

Herrera contributed musical elements, richness, color, imagery, a wealth of vocabulary, poetic language, and grandiloquence to Spanish poetry. He may be considered a founder of Gongorism, of *culteranismo.*

The natural heir of Herrera, one of Spain's best endowed poets and an artistically rich artist was **Luis de Góngora y Argote** (1561-1627), called "The Swan of Cordova." Although he has given his name (Gongorism) to a purple style in poetry, all during his life he composed songs and poems of simple popular appeal. He was particularly successful in his delicate use of the old ballad form, and his "art ballads" (*romances artísticos,* as such productions from sophisticated poets were called) are still a delight to read for their true lyric grace and charm, and for their polished expression. Góngora was always the conscientious artist, and no mere improviser. He was also celebrated and admired for his *villancicos, letrillas, décimas,* and sonnets, some of them most artfully satirical or burlesque. He did not hesitate to attack enemies like Lope de Vega and Quevedo, who answered in kind.

There are difficult or obscure passages even in Góngora's shorter poems, but it is the longer efforts which gave him the title of "Angel of Darkness," whereas in his earlier poems he was the "Angel of Light." It is most inaccurate to say that he suddenly began to seek obscure poetic corners at some particular date, though it is accurate to say that his longer poems are difficult. Yet the effort to imprison elusive poetic beauty is always discernible. His poem on the Capture of Larache (1610), his *Fábula de Polifemo y Galatea* (1612) and his unfinished *Soledades* (1613) do indeed require intense effort on the part of the reader and perhaps more poetic sophistication than most of us possess. In them the narrative is covered with a mass of ornamentation, but the decoration is truly gorgeous. They suggest the *mihrab* in the mosque, now the cathedral, of the author's native Cordova, not some simple New England church. One might disagree with Góngora's poetic methods, but few could deny that he pos· sessed extraordinary poetic genius.

There were many practicing poets in Spain in the later sixteenth century and in the seventeenth century, and few of them escaped the influence of prevailing tendencies. Lope de Vega, for example, as suggested above, was a personal enemy of Góngora, and considered himself one of the *llanos,* or plain-speakers, but there are beautiful passages in the fundamentally lyric Lope which are far from simple. He is thought of mainly as an extraordinarily fertile and gifted dramatist, but his lyrics were numerous and intensely felt, and most delicately expressed. Even if he had never written dramas, he would be considered a great lyricist, spontaneous and sincere. Even his prose works, such as his pastoral novel *La Arcadia* (1598), the religious *Los pastores de Belén,* and the autobiographical *La Dorotea* contain beautiful lyrics here and there. His long poems, epic, burlesque, religious, or didactic, now interest readers less.

The earlier **Baltasar del Alcázar,** of Seville, (1530-1606) was a poet of Epicurean tendencies, and some of his compositions are rather subtle and artificial, but more are rather simple in style. Alcázar is particularly celebrated for his festive poems, of which the best known is the *Cena jocosa*. It recounts the monologue of a gentleman who grows tipsier and tipsier as he talks of food, of drink, and of life to Inés, his companion of the evening.

Juan de Arguijo (1567-1623), of Seville, was famous for the polish of his sonnets, usually on classical themes. **Juan de Jáuregui** (1583-1641), also of Seville, poet and painter, at first opposed the *culteranos* and even wrote an *Antídoto contra las Soledades*. In his later years he himself tended more toward ornateness. **Rodrigo Caro** (1573-1647) was an antiquarian and poet, whose Latin verses are esteemed. His Spanish sonnets, especially his *Canción a las ruinas de Itálica*, show careful poetic workmanship. **Francisco de Rioja** (1583-1659), of Seville, is known for the lofty tone of his compositions, and is particularly celebrated for his poems *(silvas)* addressed to various flowers.

Esteban Manuel de Villegas (1589-1669) said that he wrote his *Eróticas* when he was fourteen and polished them when he was twenty. They are in general simple and graceful. Some of his poems are more Gongoristic. The influence of Villegas lasted through the eighteenth century.

The **Prince of Esquilache** (1577-1658), Viceroy of Peru, was a poet of note whose works are unusually free from exaggerated strivings.

The Aragonese brothers **Lupercio Leonardo** (1559-1613) and **Bartolomé Leonardo de Argensola** (1562-1631) occupied important state positions. The Argensolas are thought of as among the most classic poets of the age.

Pedro Espinosa (1578-1650), of Antequera, in his earlier years satirized Góngora and later adopted a more elaborate style himself. Espinosa is particularly remembered as an anthologist, and his *Flores de poetas ilustres de España* (first ed. 1605) gathered poems of many contemporaries, including himself.

Juan de Tassis y Peralta, second Count of Villamediana (1582-1622), was celebrated for his delicate tastes, his prodigality, and his acid tongue, and many legends have circulated about him. He was a rather fertile poet, in the elaborate manner, and some of his satirical darts in verse aimed at his contemporaries are still well remembered. He was twice banished from the Court and finally murdered. Contemporaries like Ruiz de Alarcón wrote satirical epitaphs.

Another poet who theoretically opposed but also yielded to Gongorism at moments was **Salvador Jacinto Polo de Medina** (1603-1676). His festive and satiric poems were published in 1637 under the title *El buen humor de las Musas*. **Francisco Trillo y Figueroa** (d. ca. 1660) followed Góngora rather closely, and also wrote festive poems and quite sharp satires.

Alonso Ledesma (1562-1623), **Alonso de Bonilla** and **Miguel Toledano,** all of whom published religious poems in the early seventeenth century, are thought of as great encouragers of conceptism.

Francisco de Quevedo y Villegas (1580-1645), definitely a *conceptista,* wrote profusely in prose, but he was in addition one of Spain's most fertile poets. His poems were classified under the names of all nine of the Muses, but he is particularly admirable in his extremely clever satirical verses, some of them ridiculing his contemporaries, some of them more general in scope. They are extraordinarily keen. Quevedo was also a Spaniard with real interest in conditions in his country, and he displayed high moral indignation in his famous poem addressed to the royal favorite, the Count-Duke of Olivares, in his *Epístola satírica y censoria contra las costumbres presentes de los castellanos. . . .*

The poems of the famous "preacher of kings and king of preachers" **Fray Hortensio Félix Paravicino** (1580-1633) may show more Gongoristic than conceptistic qualities, but the effect on the reader will be the same. It is a far cry from him back to the relative simplicity of the vastly superior Fray Luis de León.

The Hieronymite nun **Sor Juana Inés de la Cruz** (1651-1695) had a Spanish father but a Mexican mother, and she is properly regarded as the first literary glory of Mexico, where she was called "Tenth Muse," "*Fénix de México,*" or better. She is said to have begun to write when she was eight years old, and her numerous poems were published in three volumes. They show both Gongoristic and conceptistic modes, and are written in all sorts of verse forms. Many have real religious and lyric inspiration.

NARRATIVE POETRY

It was only natural that Spanish poets should strive to

match the epic poems of Homer, Virgil, and Ariosto. The competition was too great, and only one attempt in Spain won any real success—that of Ercilla. The remark does not apply to Portugal, whose great literary glory might be *The Lusiads* of **Luis de Camoens** (1524?-1580). It is not to be forgotten that Camoens wrote fairly numerous short poems in Castilian, mainly following the example of Boscán and Garcilaso de la Vega. He also wrote plays in Spanish.

Among those who produced long and ambitious epics may be mentioned **Alonso Hernández,** who in 1516 published his *Historia Parthenopea,* which dealt with the life and deeds of the Great Captain, Gonzalo de Córdoba; **Luis Zapata** (1526-1595) wrote an epic on the life of Charles V and entitled it *Carlo famoso,* a work more valuable as a historical document than as a literary piece; **Luis Barahona de Soto's** (1548-1595) the *Lágrimas de Angélica* or *Primera parte de la Angélica* was written in Italian narrative style, in imitation of Ariosto and was esteemed by Cervantes; **Juan Rufo** (1547?-1620) wrote *La Austríada* (1584) dealing with Don Juan de Austria; **Cristóbal de Virués** (1587) published *El Monserrate,* later recast as *El Monserrate segundo* on the legend of the founding of that monastery.

Alonso de Ercilla y Zúñiga (1533-1594) wrote what most authorities consider the century's greatest Hispanic epic. It was called *La Araucana* and was published in three parts (1569-78-89). The first part treats the conquest by the Spaniards of the Araucanian Indians of Chile, a brave and warlike people. The second and third parts dealing with contemporary events of Spanish history in Europe, such as the Battle of Lepanto, are less vigorous than the first.

Pedro de Oña (1570?-1643) was born in Araucanian territory and wrote a poem called *Arauco domado* which related the uprising of the conquered Araucanians. It is an epic attempt of some stature and may be regarded as a sort of sequel to the superior *Araucana* of Ercilla.

Ballads

The ballad or *romance,* essentially a short epico-narrative form in its origins, was of far less ambitious scope than the epics mentioned above, but ballads continued to be read and collected, and new ones produced at all periods right up to the present. Sophisticated authors who used the form have already been mentioned. Pérez de Hita's *Guerras civiles de Granada,* destined to great popularity in Spain and abroad, was particularly full of ballads, in this case *romances moriscos.* Shrewd publishers in the early seventeenth century put together a *Romancero general,* of which the first edition in 1600 contained more than 800 compositions, and the edition of 1604, in 13 parts, more than 1100. There were numerous further collections published throughout the century.

THE NOVEL

The Pastoral Novel

As the novel of chivalry declined in popularity in Spain interest in the pastoral novel began. Pastoral themes of course had been in vogue in the ancient world and the *Sicilian Idylls* of Theocritus (third century B.C.) had left their mark upon literature. Virgil himself had dealt with pastoral themes. In Italy Boccaccio's *Ameto* was famous, and was read by Spanish writers as well as by those of other countries. Jacopo Sannazzaro's *Arcadia* (1502) exercised a great influence on all Renaissance writers interested in the pastoral. In the late fifteenth century in Spain Juan del Encina (see Theater) had made use of pastoral themes and settings, and Garcilaso de la Vega had contributed to the use of the pastoral convention. Antonio de Torquemada's *Coloquio pastoril* was also a foreshadowing of the pastoral. Cervantes thought of pastorals as "books of poetry," because they all contained a considerable amount of verse.

Jorge de Montemayor (1520?-1561) gave the greatest impetus to the pastoral novel in Spain when he penned the most famous of them all in the *Diana* (ca. 1559). Montemayor was Portuguese and he had lived in the beautiful rustic setting of the Mondego River near Coimbra. He was a musician and a poet. The plot of the *Diana* is fundamentally simple: the shepherd Sireno seeks the love of Diana on the shores of the River Esla in León, but after numerous obstacles Diana marries another shepherd named Delio. The setting is idyllically pastoral, for nature is seen in its most beautiful aspects with none of its uglier realities. The characters stood for real people at court who could be recognized by the readers, for these were *"novelas de clave."* Well written in good prose and verse, the *Diana* furnished a kind of escape literature into Arcadian realms that all people have dreamed of occupying. Moreover, elements of mystery and the supernatural, magic fountains, the piping of shepherds and the bucolic, sentimentalized atmosphere made it attractive to the people of the sixteenth century.

Gaspar Gil Polo (d. 1591), whom Cervantes punningly praised (Polo-Apolo), wrote a sequel to the *Diana* in his *Diana enamorada,* supplying the happy ending which Montemayor failed to give. The plot of Gil Polo's novel is not well developed, but the style of its prose and the excellence of its poetry make up, in part at least, for this fault.

Luis Gálvez de Montalvo wrote still another pastoral, *El pastor de Fílida* (1582), which followed the convention of presenting real people disguised under pastoral names. The easy flowing style of the novel, the poetry inserted into the prose, and the general erudition of the entire work delighted its readers and won praise from men like Cervantes and Lope de Vega.

Pastorals continued to be written in the seventeenth century. The pastorals of Cervantes and Lope will be mentioned along with their more famous works.

The Moorish Novel (Novela Morisca)

The *Historia del Abencerraje y la hermosa Jarifa,* better known as the *Abencerraje,* is the first Moorish novel in Spanish. It came at a time when the Moors, no longer looked down upon or hated, were regarded as romantic characters and people to be admired. Such is the spirit of the Morisco ballads also. The story of the gallant young Abencerraje and his devoted and resourceful sweetheart, Jarifa, and of Rodrigo de Narváez, the magnanimous Spanish knight, makes a pretty story and contains simple literary excellence. It is still read with interest, and has been translated into English several times. The *Abencerraje,* itself, was inserted into the fourth book of the second and subsequent editions of the *Diana.* The best surviving version is found in the *Inventario* (1565) of Antonio de Villegas.

The Picaresque Novel (Novela Picaresca)

Like the Moorish novel, the picaresque is considered a truly indigenous creation of Spain, and its influence has been felt in that country and abroad ever since. Realistic literature had existed in antiquity, for example, *The Golden Ass of Apuleius* (first century A.D.) and *The Satyricon* attributed to Petronius Arbiter (second century). The Spanish picaresque novel had almost a formula: it is typically the real or supposed auto-biography of an "anti-hero" of humble origin, who restlessly serves various masters and who satirizes them and the life he sees about him. Society is thus viewed not from above, but from underneath. The *pícaro* is vastly different from the aristocratic knights of the novels of chivalry or the sweet masquerading shepherds of the pastorals. He is a poor little proletarian seeking fundamentally to satisfy his hunger, to escape from the sheer misery of life, from hunger, the main theme of many a Spanish literary production from the sixteenth century until now. The *novela picaresca* is indeed a novel of social protest.

The *Lozana andaluza* (1528) of Vicar **Francisco Delicado** is a completely unliterary work with strong picaresque elements. The protagonist is a girl from Andalusia who travels to Rome and lives the life of a prostitute. The novel presents a vivid picture of Roman customs in the lower strata of society. The language, colorful, racy, and colloquial, was written by a man who was a kind of *pícaro* himself. Delicado seemed proud to admit that he had experienced much of what he wrote from personal knowledge of the life he describes. (He also wrote a book on cures for syphilis.) The reputation of the *Lozana andaluza* as the most obscene book in Spanish literature is surely exaggerated.

Lazarillo de Tormes (1554) whose longer title is the *Vida de Lazarillo de Tormes y de sus fortunas y adversidades* is in many ways the greatest of the picaresque novels. It follows the picaresque formula and is told in a series of episodes in the life of the boy, Lazarillo, given first by his own mother to be the servant of a blind beggar. He serves several masters and presents a most realistic, though not bitter, picture of society in the mid-sixteenth century. The most famous episode is number three, that of the *escudero* (squire), a broken-down gentleman too proud to work, but not too proud to accept the food Lazarillo begged from the neighbors. *Lazarillo de Tormes,* the first real picaresque novel in Spanish, set the pattern and the fashion for later picaresque novels. It is one of the great Spanish classics. Its author is not known.

Guzmán de Alfarache (1599) by **Mateo Alemán** (1547-

1614?), or *Vida de Guzmán de Alfarache, atalaya de la vida humana* is the work of a man who knew the seamy side of life. Alemán was the son of a prison doctor in close contact with the petty criminals that peopled the underworld of the sixteenth century. In 1599 Alemán published the first part of *Guzmán de Alfarache* and it went through fifteen editions by 1615: a somewhat greater immediate popularity than even Cervantes enjoyed. The second part (his own, not the spurious part published in 1602) appeared in 1604. The protagonist, Guzmán, serves many masters in Spain and Italy and gives a realistic picture of life in several cities: Rome, Florence, Milan, Saragossa, Madrid, and Toledo. The picture of society as seen through this picaro's eyes is not pretty, but bitter.

An author who called himself **Francisco López de Ubeda** published *La pícara Justina* in 1605. The adventures of the heroine are less interesting than they might be. No doubt the best part of the book is in the descriptions of the region of León. The style is difficult.

The great **Francisco de Quevedo** (1580-1645) wrote his sprightly picaresque novel early in the seventeenth century, although it was not published until 1626. It is generally known by the short title of *La vida del buscón,* also as *El gran tacaño.* Quevedo was not squeamish and his view of humanity was tinged with bitterness, even with cruelty. The style is clever though complicated. The *Buscón* is definitely one of Spain's most lively and challenging picaresque novels.

El diablo cojuelo (1641) by **Luis Vélez de Guevara** (1579-1644) must be regarded as a kind of picaresque novel, although it is told in a rather different fashion from the others in this genre. A devil is able to lift the roofs of houses without disturbing the occupants. In this way one is able to observe what is going on inside and to obtain an understanding (satirical) of Spanish life. Lesage adapted Vélez de Guevara in his *Le diable boiteux* (1707).

Alonso Jerónimo de Salas Barbadillo (1580-1635), also known as a writer of *comedias* and short plays, is best known for his picaresque novel, *La ingeniosa Elena,* published in 1614. The protagonist is a picaresque lady who pretends, among other things, to be a saint. The novel *El sutil cordobés, Pedro de Urdemalas* (1620) deals also with rascality and a young man who starts a school for elegants. *Don Diego de Noche* (1623), told in the form of letters, is picaresque in tone, even if not in formula. Salas Barbadillo possessed a lively style.

Alonso de Castillo Solórzano (1584- ca. 1648), also a dramatist, produced interesting picaresque works: *Las harpías de Madrid y coche de las estafas* (1631) ; *La niña de los embustes* (1631) ; and *La garduña de Sevilla y anzuelo de las bolsas* (1642) , his best and most popular work. His writing is zestful.

CERVANTES

Spain's greatest literary genius, **Miguel de Cervantes Saavedra,** was born in Alcalá de Henares in 1547, the fourth child of seven of a struggling doctor. Really nothing is known of Miguel's early years. The record shows that around 1568-1569 he was studying in Madrid under a prominent humanist, Juan López de Hoyos, and that he wrote a couple of poems. He went to Italy in 1569, and about 1570 joined the Spanish army in Naples. His great military moment came with his participating in the Battle of Lepanto, October 7, 1571, which he always mentioned with great pride. He was wounded in the chest, and his left hand remained useless for life.

After recuperation he remained in the army until 1575, when he started back to Spain to sue for promotion. His galley was attacked and captured by Turkish pirate ships and he was taken as a slave. During his five years captivity he organized several attempts to escape, and was sentenced to 2000 lashes in 1578, but he tried again the next year. In 1580 he was ransomed and returned to Spain. He settled in Madrid, held unimportant jobs, and tried his hand at writing. A few of his plays were presented. He had an amorous intrigue with a woman named Ana Franca de Rojas, who bore him a daughter named Isabel de Saavedra.

He was working on a novel in 1584, the year of his marriage to a girl nineteen years younger than himself, with a moderate dowry. His first novel, *La Galatea,* was published in 1585.

Literature could not support him, however, and he went to Seville and engaged in a sort of brokerage business. In 1587 he secured a position as a tax and supply collector for the Spanish Armada, and he remained in government employ after the defeat in 1588. A banker with whom he deposited funds went bankrupt, and Cervantes was jailed at least twice because he could not pay. He was constantly poor.

Around 1603 he went to Valladolid and lived with some of his family there, while his wife was apparently in her native Esquivias. He was seeking permission to print a book he had been working on. Part I of the immortal *Don Quijote de la Mancha* appeared in Madrid in January of 1605, and was an immediate success. Nowadays the author would have grown rich on royalties, movie, and television rights. As it was, he remained poor all his life.

Cervantes' *Novelas ejemplares* appeared in 1613; his book of literary criticism in verse, the *Viaje del Parnaso* in 1614; *Ocho Comedias y ocho entremeses nuevos, nunca representados,* and Part II of the *Quijote* in 1615. He died in 1616. He was working on several books, but only one was published: *Los trabajos de Persiles y Sigismunda,* in 1617.

The second part of *La Galatea* was one of the books Cervantes was working on in 1616. The part published in 1585 is interesting because it states some of the author's ideas on love, which derive mainly from the *Dialoghi d'amore* of Leo Hebraeus (León Hebreo). As a pastoral novel, the *Galatea* never achieved much reputation, nothing like that of Montemayor's *Diana.* In the *Viaje del Parnaso* Cervantes lamented his lack of *"gracia"* in composing verse, and pastoral novels had to be partly in verse.

Unfortunately the early plays of Cervantes are lost, though he says that they were played "without receiving any offering of cucumbers or other throwable objects." Cervantes' *Ocho comedias* . . . (1615) have their merits. Probably the best known is the four act *La Numancia* on the famous siege of that city by Scipio Aemilianus in 130 B.C. In general Cervantes approved of plays more in accord with classical rules than those of the freer (and more poetic) Lope de Vega, whom Cervantes accused of "making off with the monarchy of the Spanish stage." True enough.

The *Entremeses* or one act *Interludes* published in the same volume interest us more. They are bright little genre paintings, scenes from life, realistic and lively. They are in the tradition of Lope de Rueda, some of whose performances Cervantes mentions seeing as a youth. The tradition of this one-act dramatic sketch was brilliantly continued by Luis Quiñones de Benavente (d. 1651) through the eighteenth century *sainetes* of Ramón de la Cruz through those of the Quintero brothers and others of the twentieth century up to our own day.

Cervantes wrote short stories at various times and at least some of the twelve published in 1613 as *Novelas ejemplares* had been written much earlier. *Novela* meant not novel but a short story on the general pattern of the Italians such as Boccaccio, Poggio, Bandello. It is true that a few, roughly translated or adapted, had appeared in print in Spain, as in the works of Juan Timoneda (d. 1583; *El patrañuelo,* 1576) and in the *Noches de invierno* (1609) of Antonio de Eslava. Yet Cervantes' claim in his preface, "Yo he sido el primero que he novelado en lengua castellana," that is, to write short stories in Spanish, is substantially accurate. He says he had called them "exemplary" because there is not one of them from which some profitable example may not be drawn. We may let the statement pass, especially since Cervantes further suggested that "there are hours when the tired spirit may rest" —in other words he thought it is justifiable to write to entertain, not merely to give moral instruction, and the stories are entertaining. Even those in which swift action is the thing, coincidence is heavily utilized and characterization neglected: *El amante liberal, La fuerza de la sangre, La señora Cornelia.* It is quite impossible here to consider all twelve in detail. Some are real bits from life, like the wonderfully presented *Rinconete y Cortadillo,* the gem of the collection. The characterization of the two little rapscallions and of the guys and dolls of the mob which they join in Seville is masterly. Monipodio, who runs the gang and who is more than once referred to by Cervantes, is quite unforgettable. *La ilustre fregona (The Illustrious Scullery-Maid)* presents a beautiful picture of aspects of life in Toledo. *El celoso extremeño* is an impressively serious presentation of the theme of the jealous and pitiable old man who marries a young wife. Cervantes would have been famous if he had written nothing except the *Novelas ejemplares.*

It happens that he also wrote the world's most celebrated and most often published novel, Part I (1605), Part II (1615). It is conceivable that Part II might not have been completed if a smart lawyer and advantage-taker who called himself **Alonso Fernández de Avellaneda** had not published a spurious continuation in Tarragona in 1614. Cervantes had reached Chapter 59 of his own work when he heard about it and he caused his own characters Don Quixote and Sancho to protest vigorously against Avellaneda's falsification.

Probably the last thing that Cervantes would have expected is the near-reverence which admiration for *Quixote* is likely to inspire. He was merely being humorous when he said he received a request from the Emperor of China to use his novel as a manual for teaching Spanish in the Chinese court. Yet *Don Quixote* has been translated in part into Mandarin, and the whole of it into forty to fifty other languages. A work must indeed have quality to be declared by so many critics the world's greatest novel. Possibly, since the popularity of the paperbacks, the remark is no longer true that the *Quixote* has been the world's most often printed book next to the Bible, but as a best seller it has lasted more than three centuries and a half thus far. How many other books have? More than that, it has entered into the spirit of many of the world's choicest novelists. The problems which it poses are not dead, since they are eternal. Each rereading of the *Quixote* suggests new meditations and new pleasures.

Thousands of pages have been devoted to the subject of just what this novel is and what it means, and all sorts of "interpretations" have been offered. Obviously it contains samples of many sorts of previous literature: Lucianesque dialogues, the pastoral, the Moorish, the short story, the picaresque, folklore, literary criticism, and most of all, the novel of chivalry, of which it is in a way a satire, a parody—the world's greatest. Yet the whole is greater than the sum of its parts. One may take it as just the story of a crack-brained oldish man who engages in silly adventures, accompanied by a gullible but shrewd and practical squire, who has, as Cervantes says, "todas las gracias escuderiles." The uncompromising idealist and the out-and-out realist, presented not separately but together and exerting their influence upon each other. The conversations between the highly cultured knight and the illiterate but smart peasant present a delightful confrontation of two points of view. Every reader realizes that he is part Don Quixote and part Sancho, and is likely to search himself to see which predominates.

Although Cervantes was perfectly aware of the cultural and spiritual preoccupations of the Renaissance, he was not trying to write any manual of systematic philosophy. Yet every episode in the novel is stimulating, and each rereading will suggest new reflections on eternally vital problems.

Cervantes took his scene and characters, nearly seven hundred of them, from the Spain of his day, but he managed to give them all a universal quality. *Don Quixote* is a book for all humanity and the world is indebted to Spain for producing it.

Cervantes' last book, *Los trabajos de Persiles y Sigismunda* (1617) is a highly idealistic Byzantine novel, which he calls a "northern history." The supposedly Scandinavian hero and heroine go through all sorts of adventures before they are happily married in Rome. If the conception is far less felicitous than that of *Don Quixote,* one nevertheless gets bright flashes of the author's creativeness and of his admirable prose style. It was influenced by the late Greek *Aethiopica (Theagenes and Chariclea)* of Heliodorus, with whom Cervantes says he ventures to compete.

THE SHORT STORY

The modern short story in Spain really begins with Cervantes' *Novelas ejemplares.* Short stories will also be found in the works of **Salas Barbadillo** (1581-1635) and **Alonso de Castillo Solórzano** (1584-1648?) , authors who emphasized the picaresque. Castillo won considerable fame for his collections, such as *Tardes entretenidas* (1625) , *Jornadas alegres* (1626) and *Noches de placer* (1631) .

María de Zayas Sotomayor (1590-1661?) , about whom very little is known, published two good collections of stories: *Novelas ejemplares y amorosas* (1637) and *Parte segunda del sarao* (1647) . Doña María was feministic in tone, and her stories were often reprinted and translated. Paul Scarron in France simply appropriated some without acknowledgment. Her style is easy and fluent, her attitude realistic. Her fiction has been called "The picaresque novel of the aristocracy."

The priest **Cristóbal Lozano** (1609-1667) wrote verse both sacred and profane, but he is especially remembered for stories contained in his prose works. His *Soledades de la vida* (1658) furnished plots for future authors. So did his *David perseguido* (1652-61) , which contains fictional episodes in addition to the life of the Biblical king.

THE THEATER

The *comedia* accomplished a synthesis of the teeming life and art of Spain's Golden Age and is a highly representative product. It combines many themes and manners: the legendary and historical, the pastoral, the picaresque, the Moorish, the fanciful, the lyric, even the religious. It is extraordinary not merely for quantity, for it is also flashingly brilliant and poetic. It was a theater for everyone, not just for the élite.

The word *comedia* was applied to any sort of full-length play, and generally signified a dramatic composition in verse, in three acts of somewhere around 1000 lines each. All sorts of verse forms were employed, and the rhythmic effects were happily varied. There was little bother about the unities, and each dramatist established his own rules of propriety. Comedy and tragedy were mingled, as they had been in the *Celestina,* or in ordinary life. The writer of plays enjoyed almost the freedom desired by romantic authors about two centuries later, but there were two entities which must be free from attack: the institution of the monarchy and the dogma of the Roman Catholic Chuch. Political liberalism and true religious freedom are still repressed in Spain at this moment. Seventeenth-century artists in Spain, however, showed no signs of chafing under restraints, but poured out their genius with a zest and brilliance matched only in Elizabethan England. France displayed greater reasonableness and higher artistic standards of composition. Italy had declined, and Germany had to wait until the eighteenth century to produce a genius of the stature of Goethe.

Juan de la Cueva (1543-1610) provided rules for drama in his *Ejemplar poético,* written late, just before he died. In it he stressed the importance of using native Spanish themes from history and legend; *la ingeniosa fábula de España.* He advocated the violation of the three dramatic unities, and the mingling of tragedy and comedy—important and long-lasting characteristics of the Spanish theater. Fourteen of his plays have survived among which are the *Siete infantes de Lara, El cerco de Zamora,* and *Bernardo del Carpio,* based upon Spanish legend and the *Infamador,* a play which some scholars used to suggest as the forerunner of Tirso's *Burlador de Sevilla.* It is not.

Andrés Rey de Artieda (1549-1613) is of lesser note and is remembered because his play *Los amantes* introduced into Spanish drama the theme of the *Lovers of Teruel,* later to be made famous. He surpassed Juan de la Cueva in weaving together his scenes. **Cristóbal de Virués** (1550-1609) wrote violent melodramas, the most startling being *Atila furioso* which has even been called *"un museo de horrores."* His *Elisa Dido,* however, contains some fine scenes, and is a work of talent. Many of his plays appear in his *Obras trágicas y líricas.* The drama of Cervantes has already been mentioned.

Lope Félix de Vega Carpio (1562-1635) was called by Cervantes "The Phenomenon of Nature," and Lope lived up to the title in every way. He was born in Madrid, of a humble family from the north. He is said to have begun dictating verses even before he knew how to write, and it is to be presumed that he began falling in love with parallel precocity. Both habits stuck with him throughout his seventy-three years. It is impossible here to give any account of the women in his life and his numerous legitimate and illegitimate children, most of whom died young. Lope was a man of passion always, and he rushed at life eagerly and incautiously and un-critically. He suffered trial, jail, and banishment for an amorous adventure begun in his 'teens, and at times he suffered remorse. He served various masters of high rank, such as the Duke of Alba and the Duke of Sessa. He was a soldier with the Spanish Armada, and wrote a poem in twenty cantos *(La hermosura de Angélica)* en route. He was ordained priest in 1614. He had already acquired the honorary title of "Familiar of the Holy Office of the Inquisition" (1609), and he belonged to four religious associations. Pope Urban VIII granted Lope a degree of Doctor of Theology and the habit of the Order of St. John (1627) ; hence his title of Frey Lope de Vega. Two years after his ordination he had one of his more violent love affairs, apparently his last great one, with Marta de Nevares. Lope was fifty-four and she was twenty-five. She went blind and then mad, and died three years before Lope. When the poet died in 1635, he had already become almost a mythical figure, and his funeral was the occasion for national mourning. One hundred and fifty-three authors contributed to a necrological volume in Madrid, and another was published in Venice. He had had many enemies in his lifetime, but many friends and still more admirers and imitators.

Lope de Vega wrote comparatively little prose, only seven or eight volumes, and only a dozen or so volumes of verse that might be called narrative or didactic. All are at least spirited and skillful. He also composed a few volumes of purely lyric poems. Prescinding from the attention that their merit deserves, one may merely pause to say that Lope was one of the greatest lyricists in the Spanish language, and the reading of many of his poems is sheer delight.

A couple of dozen volumes might constitute a satisfying life work for the average author. Lope de Vega was not average, but one of the world's most astoundingly productive geniuses. He was mainly a dramatist. His disciple Juan Pérez de Montalbán credited the master with 1800 full-length plays and 400 *autos sacramentales*. (The *auto sacramental* is a one-act play on the mystery of the Eucharist, staged on Corpus Christi Day, usually with great pomp and elaborateness.) Surely Montalbán exaggerated. Lope probably wrote only between 700 and 800 full-length plays, and an indeterminate number of one-acters. Remember that these plays were in verse, not prose; usually extraordinarily good verse. Lope himself said that there were more than a hundred which he composed in the space of twenty-four hours each. Improvisation, surely, but there is no exaggeration in saying that Lope was the most brilliant improviser that the world has yet seen. There is no point in wishing that he could have concentrated his phenomenal abilities in a few masterpieces. He could not. His gift was for exuberance, effervescence, not for concentration. Yet he produced many admirable plays, all shot through with intense lyricism, his truly great gift from the gods. He did not create great characters like Don Quixote or Hamlet or Macbeth (who has?) but he gave his audiences a good show, with plenty of plot and rapid action, and poetry like that of *Romeo and Juliet*. He really dictated the general type and technique of the romantic Spanish *comedia* of the seventeenth century.

Lope's subjects came from everywhere: the Bible, saints' lives, history, chronicles and legends, foreign and domestic, ballads, Italian short stories, contemporary life, and from his own quite sufficiently fertile imagination. His use of what we

would now call Spanish folklore material, most artistically
stylized, was noteworthy, and his delicate taste remarkable.

In such a staggeringly vast production, it would be next to
impossible to pick out, say, the ten (or twenty, or thirty)
best plays of Lope. For Biblical or religious plays, one might
try *El nacimiento de Cristo,* in three acts, but much like an
auto sacramental, or *Barlán y Josafá.* Plays on Spanish history
and legend, among Lope's best and most characteristic: *Las
famosas asturianas, El mejor alcalde el rey, El bastardo Mudarra* (on the legend of the Seven Princes of Lara) , *Audien-
cias del rey don Pedro* (which presents King Peter not as
The Cruel, but as The Justice-Dealer) , *Las almenas de Toro*
(Lope's only play which presents the figure of the Cid) ,
*Las paces de los reyes y judía de Toledo, Peribáñez, Los
Tellos de Meneses, El caballero de Olmedo, Porfiar hasta
morir* (on the legend of Macías) , *El remedio en la desdicha*
(on the charming story of El Abencerraje) , *Fuente Ovejuna.*
The last is a remarkable play in which the protagonist is a
whole town which rises and slays its cruel overlord, an action
finally justified by King Ferdinand the Catholic. Comedies
of intrigue or of contemporary manners are: *El perro del
hortelano* (which means "The Dog in the Manger") , *El
acero de Madrid, Amar sin saber a quién, La dama boba,
El anzuelo de Fenisa, La moza de cántaro, La hermosa fea,
Las bizarrías de Belisa.* They contain charming feminine
characterization, and they present amusing *graciosos.* Lope
developed the *gracioso* (clown or funny man) as an almost
obligatory feature of the *comedia,* and his actions on a lower
plane often parallel the doings of the protagonist. He serves
as confidant, jester, and realistic observer of life.

Lope de Vega could have written several full-length verse
plays in the time it takes the ordinary mortal to write a few
pages about him.

One of the better known plays of the Golden Age, formerly
but surely wrongly attributed to Lope de Vega, is *La Estrella
de Sevilla* (1623) . Its interesting but depressing plot shows
the complete loyalty of a vassal to a king (Sancho IV) who
could and did do wrong. The character of the hero, Sancho
Ortiz, is admirably portrayed.

Gabriel Téllez, better known by his pseudonym **Tirso de
Molina** (1584?-1648) , studied at Alcalá and became a Mer-
cedarian friar. He rose to high positions in his order. For

a disciple and defender of Lope, he was relatively infertile: only four hundred-odd plays, plus a few volumes of prose. We should remember, however, that he was officially stopped from writing plays when he was about forty years old, because it was alleged they gave rise to "escándalos."

Tirso wrote two miscellanies *(Los cigarrales de Toledo,* 1624, and *Deleitar aprovechando,* 1635), including stories, recitations, plays, and other means for amusement indulged in by a group of sophisticated ladies and gentlemen of leisure on country estates *(cigarrales)* near the old city of Toledo. A play included is *El vergonzoso en palacio,* one of Tirso's noteworthy *comedias palaciegas.* The bashful hero finally does very well indeed.

Tirso wrote Biblical and religious plays. *La mejor espigadera* concerns Ruth and Boaz. *La venganza de Tamar* necessarily involves incest, a theme rarely presented in the seventeenth century.

Tirso de Molina was particularly good at the *comedia de capa y espada,* the cloak and sword play, with lively intrigues and most sprightly feminine characters, and particularly funny *graciosos,* whose language and jests were very, very unrestrained. The groundlings in the pit certainly did not object, standing in the fairly rudimentary *corrales* (courtyards) which constituted Madrid's early theaters. Women sat in a balcony (called the *cazuela,* stew-pan) behind a grille, so their reactions were unobservable. Among the snappy intrigue plays of Tirso may be mentioned *Don Gil de las calzas verdes, El amor médico, Por el sótano y el torno, Desde Toledo a Madrid, Los balcones de Madrid, La villana de Vallecas, La gallega Mari Hernández. Marta la piadosa* is a fine portrait of a young woman who feigns sanctity to gain her ends and her man.

Tirso's most noted historical play is the skillful presentation of Doña María de Molina called *La prudencia en la mujer.* Some have claimed that the world's best theological play is *El condenado por desconfiado,* usually attributed to Tirso. A wicked bandit repents just before death and is saved, whereas a pious hermit doubts and is damned.

Cervantes gave the world the character of Don Quixote and Tirso the figure of Don Juan, which, in various developments, has fascinated humanity ever since: Molière, Mozart, Byron, Mérimée, Dumas, Zorrilla, Shaw, Pushkin, Pérez de Ayala, and at least scores of others. The first Don Juan Tenorio appears in Tirso's *El burlador de Sevilla y convidado de piedra*. He is a swashbuckling libertine, though no mere sensualist and pursuer of women; some dissatisfaction in his psyche causes him to seek reassurance by winning women, and abandoning them, through any sort of stratagem, as though he were taking vengeance on the eternal feminine. He is by no means anti-religious, for when his servant Catalinón repeatedly warns him of the coming Day of Judgment, he says each time "What a long time you are giving me!" He is infinitely brave, even against the supernatural powers as represented by the statue of the Comendador whom he has slain. He invites the Comendador's statue to dinner, and accepts a return engage-ment. The statue seizes Don Juan's hand and communicates to him the flames of hell. The helpless mortal pleads for confession, but the statue replies "Too late!" and Don Juan goes to his fiery doom. The theological implications are that Don Juan could have been saved if he had heeded his servant's warnings, but that there is a point beyond which God's freely offered grace is no longer operative. The Thief on the Cross had not had such previous opportunities, so his repentance was valid.

Sentimental romantics in the nineteenth century, like Zorrilla, saved Don Juan through the intercession of a woman's love, allowing him to repent even after death. Such a heterodox concept would have been completely alien to Tirso's thought.

The ugly, but proud Mexican-born hunchback **Juan Ruiz de Alarcón** (1581?-1639), universally considered one of the great dramatists of Spain's Golden Age, received an excellent education. His critical disposition was not sweetened by the jibes hurled at him by hostile authors on the score of his physical deformity, and he replied bitterly. He even referred to his theatrical audiences as wild beasts, and so addressed them in writing. His theater, far more than that of others, is one of moral and social criticism, and his careful work-manship limited his production to two dozen plays. He ceased writing when he found government employment.

Alarcón could write rip-snorting melodrama, as in *El tejedor de Segovia, Segunda parte,* or light intrigue drama such as *El semejante a sí mismo,* but he is superior in the drama of character which inveighs against general human defects. *Mudarse por mejorarse* is against inconstancy in love. *Los favores del mundo* preaches firmness amid vicissitudes. *La prueba de las promesas,* based on an excellent story of Don Juan Manuel, is a noteworthy treatment of the theme of ingratitude. *Las paredes oyen* shows the danger of gossip. The most celebrated play of Alarcón, *La verdad sospechosa,* concerns an indefatigable liar who spun himself up in his own web, to his grief. The great French dramatist Pierre Corneille had found the raw materials for *Le Cid* in the plays of Guillén de Castro. In writing the first great sophisticated French comedy, *Le menteur,* Corneille found far better than raw materials in Alarcón's *La verdad sospechosa,* which he greatly admired. It does not matter that for a long time Corneille thought the play was by Lope de Vega. Alarcón's ending, the discomfiture of the liar, seems more fitting than the pat solution of Corneille. *La verdad sospechosa* is a smooth and deft play, another tribute to the author's literary excellence and his moral earnestness.

Antonio Mira de Amescua (1574?-1644) was a disciple of Lope who felt the influence of Góngora and permitted Gongorism to color his drama. He employed, as did most dramatists of the period, well-known themes, but he was able to treat these with a good deal of originality. His *La Desdichada Raquel* is an excellent handling of the famous story of Raquel, treated also by Lope de Vega and others. Another of his better-known plays was *El esclavo del demonio,* on the 'Faust theme' of selling one's soul to the devil.

Luis Vélez de Guevara (1579-1644) wrote several types of plays: *entremeses* (*La burla más sazonada*) ; Biblical drama (*Santa Susana*) ; plays based upon Spanish history (*Más pesa el rey que la sangre,* on the theme of Guzmán el Bueno, and the famous *Reinar después de morir,* a play on the theme of the murder of Inez de Castro); non-Spanish historical plays (*El Gran Tamorlán de Persia*). The author's picaresque novel, *El diablo cojuelo,* has already been mentioned.

Luis Quiñones de Benavente (d. 1651) , friend and follower of Lope de Vega, should be mentioned along with Cervantes for his mastery of the one act *entremés.* He succeeded in making audiences laugh at his humorous and lively depictions of popular mores and psychology. Among his best *entremeses* are *El borracho* and *El marido flemático.*

Juan Pérez de Montalbán (1602-1638) was the favorite

disciple of Lope, and his imitator and biographer. Although he lost his mind and died young, we have fifty-eight plays surviving from him, with a wide variety of subjects. One was *Los Amantes de Teruel,* a legend treated by many authors from the sixteenth to the nineteenth century.

Francisco de Rojas Zorrilla (1607-1648), unlike his contemporaries, was something of a defender of the rights of women. He wrote a number of plays which are classed as tragedies, in which his style veers from the plain to the more Gongoristic. His *comedias de gracioso* may have given suggestions to Molière and some of his valets turned protagonists suggest Figaro. Rojas' most impressive play, certainly one of the Golden Age dramas most often performed down to the middle of the nineteenth century, was *Del rey abajo ninguno,* often called from the name of the hero *García del Castañar.* The theme is a development of the first title: the person of the king is sacred, but beneath the king others are on an equal footing, and a subject has a right and duty to avenge his own honor.

Guillén de Castro y Bellvís (1569-1631) was a dramatist of note, as well as a lyric poet. His fame rests mainly upon two plays about the Cid, and Corneille in France was to borrow from these plays in the composition of his famous *Le Cid,* the cornerstone of French drama. Guillén de Castro used as sources, not the *Poema de Mío Cid,* but the many ballads on the subject of the great Spanish hero. His own imagination supplied the important elements in the love affair of the Cid and Jimena. The first of these plays, known as *Las mocedades del Cid,* deals with the youthful love of the Cid for Jimena and of the events following the killing of her father by the Cid in fair combat. *Las hazañas del Cid* treats the famous theme of the siege of Zamora, when King Sancho II was killed by Bellido Dolfos.

The dramatic production of **Agustín Moreto** (1618-1669) has been called "a series of honest thefts," meaning that he quarried extensively in the plays of his predecessors. He was not the first or the last to do so. If his invention ran a little thin, his dramatic skill was considerable, and he usually improved on his models. He was little attracted by heroic subjects, but his intrigue and character plays were excellent. Examples would be *El parecido en la Corte, La confusión de un jardín, Trampa adelante.* Some of his other plays, though still remaining light in manner, have more significance, such as *No puede ser guardar una mujer, El poder de la amistad. El lindo don Diego* is an admirable presentation of a fop. A fine prescription for winning a scornful beauty by equally scornful indifference carefully trumped up by the lover will be found in *El desdén con el desdén.*

Pedro Calderón de la Barca Henao de la Barrera y Riaño, commonly called simply Calderón (1600-1681) was the last of Spain's truly great dramatists of the Golden Age. When he began his literary career in the early days of his patron King Philip IV, Spain's political power had already begun to wane, but Spanish literary creativeness had not. By the time of Calderón's death, it had, and with him the Golden Age comes to its end. His last play, *Hado y divisa de Leonido y Marfisa* is dated in 1680, though he also left an unfinished manuscript. In 1681 Calderón by request sent to the Duke of Veragua a list of his works: 110 titles. He actually wrote more.

Calderón came from a family of the petty nobility in the north, and in early youth studied at a Jesuit School, at Alcalá and at Salamanca. Calderón turned from canon law to play-writing, and he provided the public theaters and the Court with very numerous plays. He was ordained priest at mid-century, and after that wrote *autos sacramentales,* in which unusual genre he was a master, and other plays and musical dramas for the Court. His material rewards for writing, in addition to the King's favor, were far better than those of Lope or Cervantes or many others of his time.

Poetic gifts and skill made Calderón the master composer of *autos sacramentales;* some eighty of these highly poetical religious pieces have come down to us. He could even turn pagan mythology to pious use. *Los encantos de la culpa* (Ulysses and Circe) and *El divino Orfeo* (Orpheus and Eurydice) are examples. Among the best known of his *autos* are: *La vida es sueño, La cena de Baltasar, El gran teatro del mundo.* The popularity of the *autos* was a tribute to the fervent religiousness of the seventeenth century in Spain. Taste changed in the eighteenth century, and for various reasons the performance of *autos sacramentales* in Spain was prohibited by royal decree in 1765.

Calderón composed various Biblical and religious full length plays, such as *Los cabellos de Absalón, El José de las mujeres, La devoción de la Cruz, El mágico prodigioso* (St. Cyprian and the pact with the devil), *El Purgatorio de San Patricio.*

Various of Calderón's good plays are connected with history and legend, mainly Spanish. *El príncipe constante* shows the heroic devotion of Prince Ferdinand of Portugal. *La niña de Gómez Arias* shows Queen Isabella the Catholic aiding and avenging a wronged maiden. *El sitio de Bredá* dramatizes the events immortalized by Velázquez in the painting commonly called *Las Lanzas. Amar después de la muerte* is an interesting characterization of a Morisco nobleman. *La cisma de Inglaterra* gives Calderón's interpretation of the characters of Catherine of Aragon, Anne Boleyn, and the "theological and sensual king" Henry VIII. Only a slight bow to history is paid in one of Calderón's most attractive dramas, based on one of Lope by the same title and an improvement of it: *El alcalde de Zalamea.* The outraged peasant mayor Pedro Crespo executes an aristocratic captain in the royal army for having wronged his daughter, and King Philip II approves the sentence. Incidentally, Spanish audiences had by no means a French sense of stage propriety, and at the end of this play, a curtain is drawn aside and the captain is shown dead, with the garrote around his neck. The play was later performed under the title *El garrote más bien dado.* Spaniards did not flinch at horror scenes which might titillate even modern readers of certain detective fiction and "comics" *(sic),* or viewers of television.

Yet Calderón was also gifted at writing light, airy, rapid-fire, and graceful *comedias de capa y espada,* plays of intrigue in which after various amusing didoes boy gets girl amid happy wedding bells or a reasonable Spanish facsimile thereof. Such plays are *Casa con dos puertas mala es de guardar, El escondido y la tapada, La dama duende, Mañanas de abril y mayo, Los empeños de un acaso.*

It is possible that the famous sanguinary "honor" tragedies of Calderón may be better judged by understanding psychiatrists than by condemnatory modern rationalists. If it seems abhorrent to most of us that some perfectly innocent wife who has fallen under suspicion therefore must be murdered in cold blood by a husband whose personal idea of his dignity is outraged, well, all we can do is try to understand the code, and reflect on our own potential emotional violence under stress. It would probably take a large volume to elaborate on the reactions of many of us to plays like *El médico de su honra*. Similar plays which might shock us less are *El pintor de su deshonra, A secreto agravio secreta venganza,* and *El mayor monstruo los celos*. One does not know whether or not Calderón and other dramatists merely found dramatic effectiveness in situations the solution of which they might not personally have approved.

Probably the best known play abroad which has come from Spain is *Life's a Dream, (La vida es sueño,* 1635), often listed as a "philosophical drama." It is not impossible that Calderón's great poetic gift in this case may have lured many audiences and many critics into thinking that they were thinking deep thoughts. *La vida es sueño,* also utilized by the author as an *auto sacramental,* is indeed in its main plot and style a phenomenally attractive drama. What are we really like, our dreams or our everyday behavior? What is the validity of life? Life is, as the hero Segismundo says: "a frenzy, an illusion, a shadow, a fiction, and its greatest good is small, for all life is a dream, and dreams are but dreams." Calderón's "lesson" is that we should act well in this dream life, so that we may have a happy awakening in death, in a future life. The irreverent might dismiss the alleged philosophy as poppycock, but what hearer or reader can thus dismiss the lilting lines of the alluring poetry in which the concept is phrased? Calderón transports us from the terrestrial realm of sheer logic into the empyrean of poetic phantasy, and lets us happily hover there while we may.

Calderón fulfills about every requirement of any definition of the word "baroque." To take only one aspect, the author's style is definitely ornate, highly decorative, full of verbal arabesques and conceptistic curlicues, at the farthest remove from simplicity. Calderón, great poet that he was, exemplified a manner that marked the end of an age. His would-be imitators might stir his ashes but could not relight his everburning torch.

The ardent enthusiast, inspired by these lines, will later become acquainted with a great many more seventeenth-century Spanish dramatists of real worth who cannot even be mentioned here but who have at least a large handful of plays each to offer spectators then and readers now. The number from the late sixteenth century onward is surprisingly large, and many of them wrote plays which were not only esteemed but also utilized by dramatists in France and England. The Spanish *comedia,* more as a totality than for any one single play, is truly impressive.

HISTORY

A period of such historical significance as the sixteenth century called forth a number of important histories, as well as a good many that have had little influence. The discovery of the New World and its conquest and colonization afforded rich material for history, but so did events in Europe in which Spain played an active part. Jerónimo Zurita (1512-1580) wrote *Anales de la corona de Aragón;* **Ambrosio de Morales y Oliva** (1513-1591) wrote the *Antigüedades de las ciudades de España;* and **Florián de Ocampo** is well known for his faulty *Crónica general de España* (1543) utilized for plots by many dramatists. **Pero Mexía** was also a noted historian.

New World Histories

Padre Bartolomé de las Casas (1474-1566) wrote a *Historia de las Indias,* and a *Brevísima relación de la destruyción de las Indias,* sent to Charles V in 1542. He thought the Indians were endowed with all simple virtues and that they had been cruelly treated by their Spanish conquerors. It was Father Las Casas who started the "Black Legend" from which it took Spain a long time to recover. He was certainly no accurate historian.

Garcilaso de la Vega, el Inca (1540-1615) was a relative of Garcilaso the lyric poet, but his fame rests on his famous *Comentarios reales que tratan del origen de los Incas,* written in 1609, and therefore actually the property of the seventeenth century. Garcilaso was the son of a Spanish nobleman and an Inca princess, and he was reared in Peru amid the fading splendors of Inca culture and civilization. He knew and talked with his Indian relatives and acquired a great store of interesting legends and accounts. These he set down in his *Comentarios* when he was an old man living in Spain.

Spanish History

The Jesuit Father **Juan de Mariana** (1535?-1624) is still considered to be one of the greatest of Spanish historians. His works are still consulted and modern historians must include much of what he wrote. His famous history was first written and published in Latin in 1592, but it was translated into Spanish in 1601. It covers the history of Spain from early primitive times until the death of Ferdinand and Isabella. Mariana said that he was moved to put in good order all that other historians had set down, but he went much farther than this and produced a good deal of original writing. His work bears the simple title *Historia de España*.

MISCELLANEOUS PROSE

Didactic Literature

Francisco Gómez de Quevedo y Villegas (1580-1645) was a remarkable polygraph and it takes no gift of serendipity to come upon treasures in his works. He was a most copious poet, as we have said, and we have looked at his bitter picaresque novel, *El buscón*. He wrote a few plays, especially *entremeses*, and numerous religious, philosophical, political, critical, and satiric works. It is always fascinating to observe the play of his extraordinary wit.

For many, the best of Quevedo is to be found in the eight moral-satirical *Sueños* begun in 1606 but not published until 1627. It does not matter that he borrowed the free technique of the vision, the trip to Hell, from Lucian and Cicero. Quevedo violently satirizes all social classes and professions. It is hard to tell who comes out worst. Among the professions, probably doctors and their allies. Women are steadily vilified, and one suspects that Quevedo, so unlike Lope de Vega, had never known the softness of feminine love, and perhaps none of any kind. His depression over the faults and vices of mankind took the form of vigorous literary aggression. One can admire his sturdy moral earnestness, but in him one will seek in vain the broad humanity of Cervantes. Quevedo attacked the exaggerations of Góngora with his accustomed virulence, but his own style is filled with super-clever intellectual quirks which many consider equally reprehensible. He too represents late baroque tendencies.

Baltasar Gracián y Morales (1601-1658) was a keen, well-trained and embittered Jesuit, one of the literary glories of that order in Spain. His first published work was the anti-Machiavellian *El héroe,* in which the author describes twenty qualities which go to make up the personality of one who

would aspire to the title. Strangely enough, his type of *Hero*
is King Philip IV. *El político Fernando* (1640) exalts Ferdinand the Catholic. *El discreto* (1646) offers advice to one who
would get along in the world, suggesting twenty-five qualities
(realces), with a historical example of each one. *El oráculo
manual y arte de prudencia* (1647) is a collection of three
hundred maxims, and offered suggestions to La Rochefou-
cauld and La Bruyère.

The work of Gracián which most influenced his contemporaries was his *Arte de ingenio*, (1642), revised and published as *Agudeza y arte de ingenio* (1648). It favorably presents the procedures of conceptists and *culteranos*, with many
examples. Gracián made himself the preceptor of the "advanced" style.

The masterpiece of Gracián is *El Criticón* (three parts,
1651-1657), which may be called a sort of philosophical novel.
There are three divisions: youth (spring), mature age (au-
tumn), and old age (winter). Critilo, the man of culture and
reason, shipwrecked on St. Helena, there finds the completely
untutored Andrenio, the man of nature, of instinct. They
come to Spain, and observe the selfish and antisocial behavior
of men and the falseness of women. Finally they reach Rome,
contemplate the fragility of human life, and at last reach the
isle of immortality by the route of virtue and true worth. The
picture which Gracián presents of humanity is harsh, pessimistic. The style is closely packed, and one must read with
great care.

Diego de Saavedra Fajardo (1584-1648) filled important
political and diplomatic positions. His large experience is re-
flected in his best-known work, the *Empresas políticas*, or *Idea
de un príncipe político-cristiano*. An *empresa* is a kind of
emblem of hieroglyphic design, and one is placed at the head
of each chapter. The sources are mainly St. Thomas Aquinas,
the Bible, and Tacitus, and the effort to refute Machiavelli is
quite evident. Despite its somewhat overblown style, the work
was quite popular.

The *República literaria*, published seven years after the
author's death, more simply and elegantly written, presents a
vision of Spanish and foreign artists, scientists, and writers.
Moderns are startled by the omission of the *Celestina*, of
Cervantes, and of the whole of the Spanish theater. Saavedra

Fajardo considered the theater immoral, but fortunately the Spanish nation did not agree with him.

Sebastián de Covarrubias y Orozco (d. 1613) wrote the best dictionary of the seventeenth century and called it *Tesoro de la lengua castellana o española* (1611). This is a remarkable book, in spite of its omissions, for it is the best guide we have for the language of the period. It gives etymologies of words accepted in the seventeenth century, and in an effort to explain meanings, it often presents enlightening pictures of customs and strange beliefs, backed up from time to time with references and quotations from the classics of Greece and Rome.

The activities of **Vicente Espinel** (1550-1624) were varied indeed. Born in Ronda, he was a student at Salamanca, a wanderer in Spain and in Italy, probably a captive in Algiers, a poet and musician, a novelist and finally an ordained priest. It was his poetic and musical skill that made him best known in his own day, and most of his original verse was published in his *Rimas* in 1591. Posterity knows him best, however, for his semi-autobiographical, semi-picaresque novel, the *Vida del escudero Marcos de Obregón* (1618). The episodes, and the interpolated stories, anecdotes and comments are of considerable interest. Alain René Lesage made good use of the Spanish work in composing his *Gil Blas de Santillane*.

The Eighteenth Century

CRITICISM	VERSE	DRAMA	NOVEL AND MEMOIRS
Erudition	D. T. González (1733-1794)	V. García de la Huerta (1734-1787)	D. de Torres Villarroel (1693?-1770)
B. J. Feijóo (1676-1764)	N. F. de Moratín (1737-1790)	R. de la Cruz (1731-1794)	J. F. de Isla (1703-1781)
I. de Luzán (1702-1754)	José Cadalso (1741-1782)	L. F. de Moratín (1760-1868)	
	J. Meléndez Valdés, (1754-1817)		
	G. M. de Jovellanos (1744-1811)		
	M. J. Quintana (1772-1857)		
	Blanco White (1775-1841)		
	F. M. Samaniego (1745-1801)		
	Tomás de Iriarte (1750-1801)		

CHAPTER 8

The Eighteenth Century

Reigns of: Philip V, 1700-1746 (Luis I, 1724) ; Ferdinand VI, 1746-1759; Charles III, 1759-1788; Charles IV, 1788-1808; Ferdinand VII, 1808-1833 (with Napoleonic interlude).

Spain had declined in every measurable way during the sad reign of Charles II (1665-1700). The accession of the Bourbon dynasty with Philip V, grandson of Louis XIV of France, marked the beginning of a gradual rise in the quality of Spanish life, which became more evident after mid-century, as during the reign of the quite enlightened Charles III. His quite unenlightened successors strove in vain to keep the French Revolution from having its effects in Spain. Napoleon's troops were finally driven out of the Peninsula in 1814, but not long afterward Spain lost most of her possessions in the New World. The period from 1700 to 1833 was by no means one of Spain's happiest, materially or spiritually.

Spain's so-called *Siglo de Oro,* much better called her Golden Age, lasted for more than a century, and it is likewise convenient to say that the eighteenth century lasted until the death of Ferdinand VII in 1833. The period produced far more respectable scholars and critics than it did really gifted creative artists. Naturally enough, the French dynasty helped to further the dominance of French cultural ideals, some of which were inconsistent with Spain's predominantly individualistic genius. With official encouragement, however, the low level of Spanish culture was gradually raised. Even the general ideas of the French Encyclopedists and of Rousseau, likely to be regarded as highly subversive, began to make themselves felt later in the century.

CRITICISM

The learned Benedictine monk **Benito Jerónimo Feijóo** (1676-1764) spent most of his long life as a professor of theology and philosophy at the University of Oviedo. His information was wide enough to make him realize the sad state of Spanish culture by comparing it with that of foreign nations, and, though remaining within the bounds of orthodoxy, he was an assiduous enemy of superstition. His was not an age of highly specialized knowledge, and he touched almost every branch of learning in his encyclopedic *Teatro crítico universal* (8 vols., 1726-1739), supplemented by five volumes of *Cartas eruditas* (1742-1760). His statements did not pass unnoticed, and he became involved in some of the numerous philosophical and literary controversies and polemics which flourished luxuriantly throughout the century. With regard to literature, he felt that rules of composition might indeed correct extravagant abuses attributed to excessive freedom, but insisted that there was a necessary *no sé qué* for every author, and that phrase may be roughly translated as "genius."

The foremost literary preceptist of the century was **Ignacio de Luzán** (1702-1754), diplomat, scholar, and critic. His important *Poética* (1737) was based not only on the strict neoclassic opinions of Boileau, but also on the Italian interpreters of Aristotle and Horace. It refers only to compositions in verse, for the novel was not a valid art form. The efforts of Luzán and his sympathizers were praiseworthy, for they wished to correct what they regarded as unbridled literary license on the part of the less gifted successors of Lope and Calderón, and even of others. Luzán constantly urges that imagination must be curbed by reason, and that in drama the unities of time, place, and action should be duly observed, and propriety maintained. The criticism of even great playwrights of the Golden Age is not merely implied, but expressed, and that criticism was even severer in the second edition of the *Poética* (1789), published after Luzán's death. Even so, the author respects the talents of the great dramatists. He wishes they had better known and observed the rules. Toward the purpler Góngora and the conceptistic Gracián he is more severe. Other critics of the century were harsher still. There were a few, however, who championed the right of genius to follow its own dictates, a point of view quite in accord with Romantic theory and practice after 1833.

VERSE

Fray Diego Tadeo González (1733-1794) is thought of as the founder of the eighteenth-century group of poets known as the "School of Salamanca." They were connected with that university city, and they sought, mainly in vain, to revive the glories of that center when Luis de León composed his lovely poetry there. González wrote mild and graceful verse, supposedly to various charming ladies. His best-known composition is *El murciélago alevoso (The Treacherous Bat)*, in which Delio (the author) hurls rather heavy-handed invective at the little animal for frightening his delicate and lovely Mirta.

Colonel **José Cadalso** (1741-1782), widely traveled and highly cultured, met his death fighting against the English at Gibraltar. The usual statement about him is that he wrote classicism and lived romanticism. It is reported that, on leave in Madrid, he fell violently in love with the actress María Ignacia Ibáñez, and at her death tried to steal her corpse. Banished by royal order, he went to Salamanca and exerted considerable influence on other poets there. His poems, though careful in form, hardly display his real emotions. Like many others in the century, he unsuccessfully tried his hand at writing neoclassic tragedies.

His prose works can be read with greater interest. His *Los eruditos a la violeta* is a satire against affected scholars. His *Cartas marruecas,* which are no mere imitation of Montesquieu's *Lettres persanes,* give an excellent satirical picture of conditions in Spain. His *Noches lúgubres,* expressing his emotions on the death of La Ibáñez, is a true and literal example of graveyard romanticism.

The sweetest of the gentle singers of Salamanca was **Juan Meléndez Valdés** (1754-1817), who assumed the poetic name of Batilo. His depth of feeling does not equal the grace and polish of his style, but his anacreontics, eclogues, and ballads can still be read with pleasure. In later life he approached more philosophic and social themes. He displays a certain sentimentality which anticipates romanticism.

Manuel José Quintana (1772-1857), ardent patriot and earnest poet, was far more vigorous. He remained true to eighteenth-century literary standards through his long life, through all the vagaries of romanticism. He opposed Napoleon, and even the tyranny of Ferdinand VII, and suffered banishment and imprisonment, but he was restored to favor on the accession of Isabel II and died as poet laureate and Spain's grand old man. He wrote plays, one of which, though apparently strict in form, *El Duque de Viseo* (1801), is based on the style of the Gothic "Monk" Lewis. The play *Pelayo* is a commendably patriotic play, and the same note is vigorously evident in some of his poems, such as the one *To the Arming of the Spanish Provinces,* and others in 1808.

The uprising of the Madrid populace against the French in that year also inspired the excellent though violent poem *Al Dos de Mayo* of **Juan Nicasio Gallego** (1777-1853). It is a good literary companion piece to Goya's somber *Shootings of the Second of May.*

Gaspar Melchor de Jovellanos (1744-1811) was a very fair neoclassic poet and a still better patriot and citizen. His plays, such as the tragedy *Pelayo* and his sentimental drama, a *comédie larmoyante* called *El delincuente honrado,* are read by few today. Few read his compositions written under the pastoral pseudonym of Jovino, or even his earnest moral poetic satires and epistles. He shone more in his day as a statesman, patriot, magistrate, educator, economist, and general reformer, and has left us prose works bearing on themes thus suggested. A most admirable man. He was much influenced by French ideas, but he died in Asturias while being pursued by Napoleon's henchmen.

In the seventeenth century there existed in the south of Spain a group of most meritorious poets. In the eighteenth century one may speak also of a School of Seville, though less praisefully. Particularly to those of English speech, the best-known of them would be **José María Blanco y Crespo** (1775-1841), a priest who fled from Spain to England, changed his name to Blanco White and his religion from Catholic to Anglican to Unitarian, and was pensioned by the British government. In addition to highly respectable poetic and prose compositions in Spanish, he wrote an admirable sonnet in English, *Mysterious Night,* a favorite with anthologists.

Spaniards were among the first to display modern interest

in their own medieval poetry. One scholar and anthologist was **Tomás Antonio Sánchez,** who published (1779-1790) a valuable four-volume *Colección de poesías castellanas anteriores al siglo XV.* It was the first printing of the *Poema del Cid,* of Berceo, of the *Libro de Alexandre* and the *Libro de buen amor.* **Juan José López de Sedano** performed a similar service with his *Parnaso español* (9 vols., 1768-1778).

FABULISTS

La Fontaine was more or less successfully imitated in Spain by **Félix María Samaniego** (1745-1801), who began publishing his *Fábulas morales* in 1781. A more famous fabulist was **Tomás de Iriarte** (1750-1791), one of the stormy petrels in the numerous literary controversies which raged throughout the century. He wrote a long didactic poem on music, numerous pamphlets, and two very fair social comedies, but he is best remembered for his *Fábulas literarias* (1782). Many are terse and pithy and are still often quoted.

THE THEATER

Serious poets in the eighteenth century, perhaps inspired by the critical theories of Luzán and others, sought to write tragedies. Many tried, quite unsuccessfully, and their efforts were stillborn. Audiences continued to prefer Golden Age plays, either in their original form or slightly more regularized in adaptations *(refundiciones).* **Cándido María Trigueros** (1736-1801?), for example, turned *La Estrella de Sevilla* into a five-act *Sancho Ortiz de las Roelas,* and recast some plays of Lope. The later **Dionisio Solís** (1774-1834) adapted numerous plays, several for the great actor Isidoro Máiquez. Audiences demanded life and action, and were willing to patronize even very inferior dramas like those of **Luciano Francisco Comella** (1751-1812).

The only tragedy of the century which has really survived is *La Raquel* (1778), by **Vicente García de la Huerta** (1734-1787). It is based on a popular Spanish historical episode, the love of Alfonso VIII for the Jewess of Toledo, already treated by Lope de Vega in *La Judía de Toledo,* and it is in three acts, not five. Being in 11-syllable assonating lines, it has not the metrical variety characteristic of Golden Age plays, but it could be readily accepted by those who could not stomach neoclassic tragedies.

Nicolás Fernández de Moratín (1737-1780) wrote three thoroughly unsuccessful tragedies, but he did write one of the century's most attractive poems, *La fiesta de toros en Madrid,* which has really romantic color and verve.

A much more famous dramatist was his son, **Leandro Fernández de Moratín** (1760-1828). His principles were neoclassic, but he got around to translating *Hamlet,* rather disapprovingly. He also translated Molière, who was the chief model for the younger Moratín's five comedies. He had dramatic skill, and his *La comedia nueva o el café* (1792) is an amusing satire of bad plays produced in his time, like those of Comella. To some it is more valid than Moratín's most famous play, which has aged badly: *El sí de las niñas* (1806). It fairly amusingly teaches the lesson that parents and older relatives should not exert undue authority in arranging the marriages of the young. The dialogue is lively, and the character of the mother, Doña Irene, is comically portrayed. Moratín also wrote a sort of history of the drama called *Los orígenes del teatro español,* which can still be consulted with profit. His lyric poems are less winsome.

Ramón de la Cruz (1731-1794) was truly Spanish in his realism and in his fecundity: 69 tragedies, comedies, and musical plays, including translations, and 473 *sainetes,* short "slice of life" pieces showing true comic verve. They are in the tradition of the *pasos* of Lope de Rueda and the *entremeses* of Quiñones de Benavente and Cervantes, and give a bright and pleasantly satirical picture of Spanish life in the eighteenth century, high, low, and middle. The emphasis on local color anticipates the later romantics, and the *sainetes* are in a class with the brilliant cartoons of Goya. Those two artists stand out in a century which in Spain was mainly academic rather than bright. A few typical examples are: *La Plaza Mayor por Navidad, Las castañeras picadas, El petimetre, El Rastro por la mañana, El Prado por la noche, Las tertulias de Madrid, La presumida burlada, La comedia casera, El teatro por dentro, El sainete interrumpido.*

NOVEL AND MEMOIRS

Dignified authors in the eighteenth century did not care

to write novels, and the tradition of the picaresque, and of other forms too, became practically extinct. The Jesuit Father **José Francisco de Isla** (1703-1781) was a mild exception. His *Historia del famoso predicador Fray Gerundio de Campazas, alias Zotes,* is a long and not too lively satire of bombastic preachers and their devices for impressing their congregations. The chief work of Padre Isla was a translation, of the *Gil Blas de Santillana* of Alain-René Lesage. Since Lesage translated several Spanish picaresque novels and utilized others in his own work, Padre Isla was in spirit though not literally accurate in suggesting that he was restoring the novel to its original language. The translation is free, colloquial, and lively and showed that the translator was capable of writing good, natural Spanish prose, which is still read with pleasure today.

Diego de Torres Villarroel (1693-1770) was a university professor, but not quite a conventional one. He was also, at various times, a street singer and dancer, bullfighter, beggar, false hermit, soldier, quack doctor, lockpicker, poet, churchman, and philanthropist. He was a slightly restless type, but a real reformer who realized the need of reform in Spain, not from reading, but from direct contact with an unusual number of the phases of Spanish life. The most important of his rather numerous works is his *Vida* (1743). It may be slightly mendacious in spots, but it is not dull. Torres' model for style seems to have been Quevedo, and the *Vida* might be considered a sort of picaresque novel in itself.

Romanticism

POETRY	DRAMA	NOVEL	*COSTUMBRISMO* (Criticism)
Duke of Rivas (1791-1865)	F. Martínez de la Rosa (1787-1862)	Translations and Imitations of Sir Walter Scott.	R. Mesonero Romanos (1803-1882)
Juan Arolas (1805-1849)	Duke of Rivas (1791-1865)	Larra, *El doncel* (1834)	S. Estébanez Calderón (1799-1867)
José de Espronceda (1808-1842)	M. J. de Larra (1809-1837)	Espronceda, *Sancho Saldaña* (1834)	M. J. de Larra (1809-1837)
N. Pastor Díaz (1811-1863)	J. E. Hartzenbusch (1806-1880)	Gil y Carrasco, *El Señor de Bembibre* (1844)	
G. Gómez de Avellaneda (1814-1873)	A. García Gutiérrez (1813-1884)	M. Fernández y González (1821-1888)	
José Zorrilla (1817-1893)	José Zorrilla (1817-1893)	E. Pérez Escrich (1829-1872)	
G. A. Bécquer (1836-1870)	M. Bretón de los Herreros (1796-1873)		
Rosalía de Castro (1837-1885)			
E. Gil y Carrasco (1815-1846)			

CHAPTER 9

Romanticism

Queen: Isabel II (1833–1868)

Since Isabel II was only a baby when Ferdinand VII died in 1833, Queen María Cristina and her ministers were in charge, and were forced to adopt a somewhat liberal attitude to combat the claim to the throne of Ferdinand's brother Don Carlos, who rose in arms with his conservative supporters. The First Carlist War was settled in 1837, but no great political or material progress was made. Spain figured very little in international affairs.

Romantic authors in Spain displayed the same characteristics that existed elsewhere in Europe: subjectivity, individualism, freedom from restraint and rules, a greater interest in nature, a seeking for picturesqueness, the dominance of emotion over reason, a tendency to go to the Middle Ages for subjects, to seek local color. Foreign influences in Spain were important: Italy, Germany, England, and especially France. Translations flooded the country. Young's *Night Thoughts,* Thompson's *The Seasons,* Mac-Pherson's Ossianic prose poems helped to create a sentimental mood and a new attitude toward nature. Sir Walter Scott was widely read, esteemed, and imitated. Byron was admired. Rousseau, Chateaubriand, and various minor French novelists, Victor Hugo, and Dumas the Elder were extremely well known. The last two and Eugène Scribe almost dominated the Spanish theater. Goethe's *Werther,* first translated in 1803, helped to produce a generation of sad or even suicidal young men. Sentiment and sentimentality were cultivated on principle. Many young Spaniards, in exile from the oppressions of Ferdinand VII, traveled or lived abroad, especially in England and France, and became familiar with the literary patterns followed in those countries. One must not forget the relative freedom of the Spanish Golden Age. Romanticism was regarded by some Spaniards as a return to a native tradition.

It is convenient to date nineteenth-century romanticism in Spain as beginning at the death of Ferdinand in 1833 and to say that it continued until after mid-century. The exiled liberals returned in 1833, bringing their new theories with them.

VERSE

One of the exiles who returned was **Angel de Saavedra** (1791-1865), later **Duke of Rivas.** He was born in Cordova, and his education and his early and not noteworthy works were neoclassic. He was noble, rich, and liberal in politics, and fought against the French in the Napoleonic wars. Banished by Ferdinand in 1823, he spent five years of exile on the island of Malta. There the cultivated Englishman John Hookham Frere introduced him to English literature, including Byron and Scott. In 1828 Rivas wrote a poem, *The Lighthouse of Malta (El faro de Malta),* which is decidedly romantic. He later spent some years in France.

Returning to Spain in 1834, when he succeeded to the title of Duke of Rivas, he published a romantic epic poem based on the old Spanish ballad legend of the Infantes de Lara, called *El moro expósito o Córdoba y Burgos en el Siglo X.* It is preceded by a preface by Alcalá Galiano which constitutes a sort of romantic manifesto. It is not noted for vivid narration, but Rivas was a painter, and many of the descriptions are brilliant. The *Romances históricos,* published together in 1841, display the same qualities of color and picturesqueness, but are better narratives in verse.

Of the violent drama *Don Alvaro* (1835), we shall speak later. The Duke grew much more conservative with age, and devoted himself mainly to affairs of state.

The poet **José Zorrilla** (1817-1893), small in stature but ambitious in utterance, is often called the spoiled darling of Spanish romanticism. He began early and poured forth an unending stream of gushing verse for nearly three generations. His one attempt at the epic was his unfinished *Granada.* His verse *Leyendas* are far better, and he gave final form to many a Spanish legend as it is known today. In all his works, he claims, two ideas are uppermost: his motherland and his religion. He dashed off countless poems of the sort popular everywhere during romanticism: *Orientales,* showing a strong influence of Victor Hugo, poems to the moon, to gray, sunless days, to various beautiful women, etc. His thought is negligible, for he was one of the least intellectual of poets, but his imagery, though not particularly original, and his descriptive powers are noteworthy. His true gift was for melody. He may not say much, but he says it always with a gorgeous and truly mellifluous lilt.

These gifts are also displayed in his numerous and highly popular dramas, of which more anon.

José de Espronceda (1808-1842) is often though somewhat inaccurately called the Spanish Byron. His stormy life included violent political activities in his teens, fighting at the barricades in Paris, and the abduction of his beloved though already married Teresa Mancha, with whom he lived passionately and brawlingly until she died of tuberculosis like a true romantic heroine.

Espronceda, like many others, was taught by the neoclassic and moderate Alberto Lista, and his early and not very successful poems were in that vein. During his short life he wrote some of the most intensely romantic poems in the language, regularly with dominant notes of sadness, disillusionment, despair, and often sardonic protest. The scholar and critic Adolfo Bonilla has summarized Espronceda's philosophy thus: the first principle of life, doubt; the chief reality, pain; the only solution, death. One of his most characteristic short poems is *A Jarifa en una orgía,* which is bitter, cynical, disillusioned, suggesting that one end "en un letargo estúpido y sin fin." Espronceda loved to portray antisocial types: *El verdugo, El mendigo, El reo de muerte, El canto del cosaco.* The grandiose *Himno al sol* is Ossianic in inspiration. Espronceda was an extraordinarily skillful versifier, and his famous *Canción del pirata* is a metrical tour de force. The metrical variety is astonishing, too, in the much longer sort of *leyenda, El estudiante de Salamanca.* It portrays a young libertine who witnesses his own funeral, but dances off with his skeleton bride with the same romantic swagger that he had displayed in life.

El diablo mundo (1841) is an attempt at a sort of epic of humanity. The hero, a rejuvenated Adam, finds new reasons for disillusionment in all classes of society that he encounters. The second of the six cantos (the poem was unfinished) is a heartfelt and deeply lyric portrayal of the poet's experiences with his Teresa. When the romantic chaff in Espronceda is swept away, there still remains a true essence of lyric feeling and expression.

The pathetic career of the Valencian priest **Juan Arolas** (1805-1849) ended in insanity. He did a great deal of literary hack work, and published good volumes of verse, notably *Poesías* (1840-43), and long after his death his poems were gathered together as *Poesías religiosas, caballerescas, amatorias y orientales* (1860, 3 vols.). His religious poems seem fervent and sincere, his *Orientales* and love poems seem to reflect a desire to escape from a profession for which he had no vocation. He displays the influence of various poets, Byron, Hugo, Lamartine, the Duke of Rivas, Zorrilla, and others.

Enrique Gil y Carrasco (1815-1846), who died of tuberculosis in Berlin, is probably best known for a historical novel concerning the last days of the Knights Templar in Spain called *El Señor de Bembibre,* but he was also a lyric poet. He is especially remembered for a sweet little poem called *La violeta,* melancholy and gentle as the author.

Nicomedes Pastor Díaz, (1811-1863) was a sentimental Galician who spent most of his life as a politician. He was also a poet, and his *Poesías* (1840), delicate, sentimental, and melancholy in tone, show the characteristics usually associated with Galicia and Portugal.

Gertrudis Gómez de Avellaneda (1814-1873), a Cuban who came to Spain in 1836, was much more vigorous in her poems and dramas. A contemporary said of her: "Es mucho hombre esta mujer." Her religious and amatory poems show vigor and sincerity. She is especially esteemed for her mastery of long verse lines, up to sixteen syllables. She was also a dramatist and novelist. Her play *Baltasar* (1858), based on the Book of Daniel, is very robust in tone, and was quite successful. Her novel *Sab* (1841), antislavery, is often called "The Spanish *Uncle Tom's Cabin,*" though the comparison is not quite exact.

Two late romantic poets, not enormously esteemed in their own day, seem to have steadily grown in critical esteem, while the glories of the highly popular Zorrilla and the later Campoamor have been seriously tarnished. One is the Galician daughter of a priest, **Rosalía de Castro** (1837-1885). Her illegitimate birth, and perhaps her marriage to a somewhat plodding and impecunious historian, Manuel Murguía, and the death of her youngest son, seemed to sadden her, and her poems, in Galician and in Castilian, are extremely melancholy in tone. The sadness is obviously real and not trumped up according to some romantic formula. The expression is melodious. She published her *Cantares gallegos* (1863) and *Follas novas* (1880) in Galician, her *En las orillas del Sar* (1884) in Spanish. The last has been delicately translated by Professor S. G. Morley (*Beside the River Sar*, Berkeley, 1937). The request made by the poet that all surviving unpublished manuscripts should be destroyed was actually carried out by her daughters and a priest. She is now held in greater esteem than at any time during her life, and some actually consider her the greatest poet of nineteenth-century Spain.

Gustavo Adolfo Bécquer (1836-1870) came from sunny Seville, but there is no Andalusian sunlight in his works. His short life was a struggle against poverty, neglect, and disease. He and his beloved brother Valeriano both died of tuberculosis. Bécquer went through an unhappy marriage, and was unloved by the woman who most attracted him.

Bécquer's nature was dreamy and sentimental, and he had a penchant for the eerie, the mysterious, the fantastic, like the German Hoffmann. These qualities show in his prose *Leyendas*, vastly different from those of Zorrilla. Bécquer's reputation comes from his relatively small volume of *Rimas*, not published together until the year after the poet's death. In the first *Rima* Bécquer expresses his desire to write the world's "gigantic and strange hymn . . . taming wretched, petty language with words which would be sighs and laughter, colors and musical notes," and he nearly achieves his ideal— far more sighs than laughter. He is one of those rather rare poets who have enormous appeal both to sophisticates and to the populace. The *Rimas* constitute a melancholy history of the poet's sentimental life, simply expressed but delicately wrought. Many of the poems are known by heart by most Spaniards, such as *Volverán las oscuras golondrinas, Cerraron sus ojos, Del salón en el ángulo oscuro,* and others. Their melancholy sentimentality is sincere and unashamed, expressed with real artistry.

There were numerous minor poets during romanticism, as there have been at all periods of Spanish history.

THE NOVEL

The "original" novels of the eighteen-thirties and 'forties in Spain did not amount to much. Apparently all novelists of the time who did not translate Sir Walter Scott closely followed and imitated him, though they spread on their pages lots of murky gloom foreign to the sturdy Scotchman. One of the least bad is *El doncel de don Enrique el Doliente* (1834). The hero is the famous Galician troubadour Macías, and the author, far more gifted as a critic, is **Mariano José de Larra** (1809-1837). The sad *Sancho Saldaña* (1834) by **Espronceda** adds little to the poet's glory. Some consider **Enrique Gil**'s *El señor de Bembibre* (1844) the best novel of the time. It is picturesque, but very languid.

Manuel Fernández y González (1821-1888) is called the Spanish Dumas mainly because he dashed off some five hundred volumes of novels. (Dumas claimed twelve hundred.) The Spaniard based his works mainly on themes from Spanish history and legend. He proved that fecundity is not a wholly unmitigated blessing.

Another cultivator of the *feuilleton* was the very popular **Enrique Pérez Escrich** (1829-1897). His highly moral tales show him to be greatly in favor of faith, hope, and charity.

THE DRAMA

The *comedia* of Spain's Golden Age was in a general sense more romantic than classic, but the romantic melodramatic stage productions of the 1830's and 1840's were based on a congeries of ideas which would have horrified Lope de Vega or Calderón. Hugo and the elder Dumas were the chief models. Their plays were put on in translation, and they were imitated. The "original" plays in Spain in the earlier nineteenth century were in Spanish, but with a Dumasesque accent. Occasionally there was a bow to other French thrillers like Ducange, Caigniez, Pixerécourt, Delavigne, with another bow to Scribe for the comedy.

Francisco Martínez de la Rosa (1787-1862) spent his exile after 1823 in France, and was converted to romanticism.

He even put on a mildly romantic play in Paris, *La révolte des Maures sous Philippe II* (1830), not played in Madrid until 1836, with the title *Aben Humeya*. On his return to Madrid, he presented the first native romantic drama, *La conjuración de Venecia,* with blobs of local color, a cemetery (pantheon) scene, Venice at carnival, the Council of Ten, conspiracies, a glamorous hero of unknown origin who is finally sentenced to death by his own suddenly recognized father, and a sweet, willowy heroine who goes mad after her lover is executed. The play is in prose.

The year also saw the production of Larra's *Macías,* in verse, on the same theme as the author's novel *El doncel.*

In 1835 appeared *Don Alvaro, o la fuerza del sino,* in mixed prose and verse, by the **Duke of Rivas.** It is familiar to opera goers as Verdi's *La Forza del Destino,* and it is a romantic play to end them all, almost like a caricature of itself. It has everything except good sense and moderation. The *sino* or fate consists of a completely implausible series of accidents and coincidences. There is much local color in the form of popular scenes, and humor and tragedy are stirred in the same pot. The innocent heroine is stabbed to death by her irate and vengeful brother, who is stabbed by Don Alvaro, who plunges to his death over a cliff, after screaming "Curses! Extermination! Perish the human race!" while the chapel bells toll, the lightning flashes, and the thunder roars. If you are in the mood, it is all thoroughly delightful.

Verdi used another Spanish play for *Il Trovatore*: *El trovador* by **Antonio García Gutiérrez** (1813-1884). It is also in mixed prose and verse. The heroine, named Leonor like so many romantic heroines, is still sweet, but this time she is a rather more vigorous type. The doughty hero Manrique thinks he is the son of a Gipsy, but he is, naturally, the long-ago-abducted brother of the villain, don Nuño, who wishes to marry Leonor. Don Nuño is informed of his brother's identity just after he has had his executioner lop off Manrique's head. Leonor has, of course, taken poison. García Gutiérrez wrote sixty or so more plays. *Simón Bocanegra* was also utilized by Verdi. Gutiérrez scored another triumph as late as 1864 with *Venganza catalana.*

Juan Eugenio Hartzenbusch (1806-1880) was the son of a German cabinet maker established in Madrid, whose real penchant was for learning and who ended as Director of the

National Library and published a great deal of scholarly work. He also wrote numerous plays of all sorts. His most noteworthy drama is the highly romantic *Los amantes de Teruel* (1837). It is based on an often used and supposedly Spanish legend which is really a hispanization of the *Decameron* story of Girolamo and Salvestra. The play is in verse. The hero finds his promised bride Isabel already married to the villain when he is delayed in returning. He suddenly dies of a broken heart, and Isabel expires on his corpse.

The most popular of the romantic dramatists was the poet **José Zorrilla.** His first stage success came in 1840, with the first part of *El zapatero y el rey,* on the legend of King Peter I (The Cruel, though presented on the stage of the Golden Age and later as The Justice Dealer). Zorrilla's *El puñal del Godo* is a good dramatic presentation of the legend of Roderick the last of the Goths. In 1844 Zorrilla wrote Spain's most popular play, still presented around All Souls Day in all parts of the Spanish speaking world. It is *Don Juan Tenorio,* all in ringing verse, one of the most poetic treatments of the Don Juan legend. Zorrilla's heroine Doña Inés, of whom he was very proud, is in reality a pretty silly little adolescent of sixteen summers, and his Don Juan, a swashbuckling bad boy who, on a bet, kills thirty-two men in duels and seduces seventy-two ladies in one year, and carries certified lists to prove it. The best line in the play is uttered by Don Juan's rival Don Luis: "¡Es increíble, Don Juan!" The play none the less has spirit, zest, rapid movement, and, chiefly, gorgeous verse to save it from its deserved fate. The romantics could not bear to drag so brave and glamorous a figure down to hell as did Tirso de Molina, Molière, and Mozart in their Don Juan dramas. This time he is saved, after his death, because of the love and intercession of his victim Doña Inés, and their souls are seen by the audience to issue from their mouths and fly up to heaven.

Zorrilla wrote many other plays, of which the best is *Traidor, inconfeso y mártir* (1849). It is an excellent treatment of the legend of Sebastian, the lost king of Portugal, killed in Africa in 1578.

There were many other dramatists, and the theatrical fare offered was varied indeed. It must never be thought that only romantic plays were shown during what we are pleased to call the romantic period.

Manuel Bretón de los Herreros (1796-1873) should at least be mentioned. He tried his hand at romanticism, but gave it up for the production of mainly realistic and mildly satirical pieces which display good observation and a sense of humor. His inspiration was mainly Moratinian, as shown in the first play he wrote, *A la vejez, viruelas* (1824). His best-known play, a jolly satire of bourgeois types, is probably *Marcela, o ¿cuál de los tres?,* in which a young widow rejects the suits of three amusingly characterized suitors.

COSTUMBRISMO. CRITICISM.

The sketch, depicting customs and manners, was a recognizable form in the seventeenth century, and Cervantes' *Rinconete y Cortadillo* might be offered as an ideal sample of the genre. Nineteenth-century Spaniards were familiar with Addison and Steele's *Spectator* and *Tatler,* and with the productions in France of Étienne Jouy and L. S. Mercier. The genre is connected with romanticism in the aspect of local color, and the presentation of popular types. The articles ordinarily appeared first in newspapers and magazines, and their authors are known as *Costumbristas*. The most characteristic of them was **Ramón de Mesonero Romanos** (1803-1882), a comfortable and well-fed *bon bourgeois* with a keen eye and a humorous slant on life. He published his numerous and excellent sketches in several Madrid newspapers, such as *Cartas Españolas, El Español* and *El Semanario Pintoresco Español*. They were later gathered together in book form as *Panorama Matritense, Escenas Matritenses,* and *Tipos y Caracteres*. He also wrote about his beloved home town in *El antiguo Madrid,* and wrote his memoirs under the title *Memorias de un setentón, natural y vecino de Madrid*. All still possess vitality, grace, and charm, and can be read far more easily than the depressing romantic novels. Mesonero called himself *El Curioso Parlante*.

Serafín Estébanez Calderón (1799-1867), *El Solitario,* was the portrayer of his native Andalusia and its colorful scenes and doings. He unfortunately adopted a somewhat antique and complicated prose style, but his descriptions are vivid. He is chiefly known for his *Escenas andaluzas,* gathered together in 1847.

Mariano José de Larra, "Fígaro" (1809-1837) was educated mainly in France. He was a professional journalist, and became the highest-paid newspaper man of his day. He had an insoluble conflict between head and heart, and committed suicide over a love affair at the age of twenty-eight.

Although Larra wrote keen and delightful satirical articles about the contemporary scene, it would be a grave error to think of him as a mere *costumbrista*. He was one of Spain's best literary and general critics of all time. His wit was mordant, and he turned it unreservedly on any victim. He was deeply aware of the faults of individuals and of the Spain of his day: the lack of culture, sloppy political behavior, lack of ideals, the constant disorders, indifference toward all vital issues, and general human stupidity and malice. His literary criticism is most perspicuous, and his articles of all sorts hit deep, and increased in bitterness as his own personal depression increased. Many consider his prose style the best in Spain after Cervantes.

A legion of Spaniards wrote *costumbrista* articles. An enterprising publisher got practically all known Spanish writers to contribute to a volume called *Los españoles pintados por sí mismos* (1843). Its sequel was, naturally, *Las españolas pintadas por sí mismas*.

These articles furnished the basis or background for the later realistic novel. The fairly numerous so-called historical novels written in Spain during romanticism were relatively pale imitations of Sir Walter Scott. The authors were likely to be known better for work in other fields. We have mentioned as examples: Larra, *El doncel de don Enrique el Doliente* (1834) ; Espronceda, *Sancho Saldaña* (1834) ; Gil y Carrasco, *El Señor de Bembibre* (1844).

The Nineteenth Century: Second Half

The Nineteenth Century: Second Half

NOVEL	VERSE	DRAMA	ORATORY, HISTORY, SCHOLARSHIP
Fermán Caballero (1796-1877)	R. de Campoamor (1817-1901)	A. López de Ayala (1828-1879)	E. Castelar (1832-1899)
Juan Valera (1827-1905)	G. Núñez de Arce (1832-1903)	J. Echegaray (1832-1916)	J. Costa (1846-1911)
P. A. de Alarcón (1833-1891)		M. Tamayo y Baus (1825-1881)	P. de Gayangos (1809-1897)
J. M. de Pereda (1833-1921)			M. Menéndez y Pelayo (1856-1912)
E. Pardo Bazán (1852-1921)		B. Pérez Galdós (1843-1920)	
L. Alas (1852-1901)		J. Dicenta (1863-1917)	
A. Palacio Valdés (1853-1928)			
B. Pérez Galdós (1843-1920)			
V. Blasco Ibáñez (1867-1928)			

CHAPTER 10

The Nineteenth Century, Second Half

Isabel II, 1833-1868. Provisional Government, 1868-1870. Amadeo I, of Savoy, 1870-1873. First Republic, 1873-1874. Restoration, Alfonso XII, 1874-1885. Alfonso XIII, 1886-1931.

Spain hardly shared in the benefits of the Industrial Revolution, and her economic progress in the nineteenth century was not great. Politically the forms of constitutional monarchy were theoretically adopted and practically not realized. The government was controlled by a series of strong military leaders. Queen Isabel II, partly because of her irregular personal conduct, was dethroned in the September Revolution of 1868. Amadeo of Savoy, invited to the throne in 1871, felt forced to abdicate the next year. The First Spanish Republic, 1873-1874 was unsuccessful, and Isabel's young son Alfonso XII was put on the throne in 1874. The last Carlist War was ended in 1876, and a new Constitution was proclaimed. Political difficulties remained unsolved even during the minority of Alfonso XIII (b. 1885), and worsened during his reign, until 1931. Observant authors like Galdós were well aware of Spain's many problems, which have not yet reached a satisfactory settlement.

REALISM

Romanticism is ever with us, but as a self-conscious movement, characterized by exaggerated literary and vital behavior, it was relatively short-lived in Spain as elsewhere. Around the middle of the nineteenth century other tendencies manifested themselves, notably a movement toward realism. We have observed that literary periods always overlap.

The sketches on manners, usually short, were developed into larger *cuadros de costumbres,* giving the authors more scope. To form a novel, all that was needed was to superimpose a plot on such a background, and that is precisely what was done at mid-century.

THE REALISTIC REGIONAL NOVEL

Cecilia Böhl von Faber (Böhl de Faber) (1796-1877) was the daughter of Johan Nikolas Böhl von Faber, who was Consul from Hamburg to Cadiz and a great lover and defender of Spanish literature. Born in Switzerland, educated in Germany, mainly in the French language, the daughter returned to her mother's native Cadiz and became enormously interested in the character and the doings of her fellow Andalusians. She showed that interest in Spain's first nineteenth-century regional novel by publishing *La Gaviota* (1849), which she had originally written in French. Because she feared literary works by a woman would be disesteemed, she took the pseudonym of "Fernán Caballero," the name of a village in La Mancha, and by that name she is always known.

The plot, characterization, and literary style of *La Gaviota* are unremarkable, but the portrayal of the folkways of simple Andalusians in the first part is attractive and successful. Fernán Caballero is sentimental, unsophisticated, and an arch-conservative in her ideas, but she is the real precursor of a large group of far better novelists who followed her lead. Despite her three not too happy marriages, she found time to write a great many more novels displaying her interest in her folk. Among the most popular were *La familia de Alvareda, Clemencia, Lágrimas* and *Un servilón y un liberalito.* Fernán Caballero tried to do for Spain what George Sand did for the people of Nohant, in her section of France.

The aristocratic **Juan Valera** (1827-1905) combined the most cosmopolitan, urbane, and cultured qualities to be found in the Spain of his day. He traveled widely as a diplomat, including a stay in Washington, but he found time to write voluminously in various genres, including literary criticism which was penetrating but likely to suffer from excessively well-bred benevolence. His plays and poems are now forgotten, and he is mainly thought of as one of the most important of the novelists who began writing in the eighteen-seventies.

Valera bore practically no resemblance to Fernán Caballero except that they were both Andalusians, and the sun-kissed south of Spain is the scene of their important works. Valera's first and definitely most important novel was *Pepita Jiménez* (1874), which portrays the emotional gyrations of a young seminarist who comes home to his unnamed little Andalusian town just before his ordination and meets the charming young widow Pepita. She, aided by nature in the springtime, persuades him that his mysticism was hollow, so they marry and settle down to a fine patriarchal life. The charms of village life as described by Valera are about equal to those of his heroine, and his realism never extends to anything really unpleasant. The elegance of the author's style is enhanced by his gentle skepticism. He referred to his ideal of a "pretty" novel, and *Pepita Jiménez* is indeed like a Watteau and not violent like a Goya *capricho*.

Andalusia is also the background of other novels by Valera, such as *El Comendador Mendoza* (1877), *Pasarse de listo* (1878), *Doña Luz* (1879) and *Juanita la Larga* (1895). *Las ilusiones del doctor Faustino* (1875) presents a modern Dr. Faustus, and *Morsamor* (1899) tends toward the fantastic.

Valera's polished style has stood the test of time better than that of any of his contemporaries.

An Andalusian of far less culture, elegance, and restraint is **Pedro Antonio de Alarcón** (1833-1891), all but one of whose exuberant novels have dated very badly. He produced his first melodramatic thriller, *El final de Norma* at the age of eighteen, and he showed no particular signs of precocity. He wrote a number of short stories, some of which are still very readable. The background of most of his works is his native Andalusia. That is true of his best novel, really a long short story, *El sombrero de tres picos* (1874). It is a somewhat bowdlerized retelling of a story contained in ballads concerning *El molinero de Arcos,* and is filled with rollicking humor, zest, vivid narration, and pleasant, broad caricature. Manuel de Falla made it into a delightful ballet. Other novels by Alarcón, marred by trumped-up intensity, melodramatic didos, and excessive verbosity, are *El escándalo* (1875), *El niño de la bola* (1880), and *La pródiga* (1881). Alarcón also wrote some good travel books. He was a born story-teller, but lacked delicacy and a sense of proportion.

José María de Pereda (1833-1905) was born the same year as Alarcón, but in very different circumstances and at the opposite end of the country: the province of Santander. That city, the sea before it, and the mountains behind it form the setting for most of this noble old hidalgo's novels. Spaniards call the region *La Montaña,* and Pereda is its chief chronicler. He gave up his training as an artillery officer, returned to his beloved home, and devoted himself to writing, first short sketches and then full-fledged novels. His ideas are always superconservative, and he constantly champions the good, old virtues, conventional traditional ideas in church, state, and personal behavior. His first novel, *El buey suelto* (1878) was written to show the wrongness of Balzac's *Physiologie du mariage* and *Petites misères de la vie conjugale.* It is not a very good novel. Better is *Pedro Sánchez* (1883), which condemns the career of a shifty politician and the corrupting atmosphere of cities, where craftiness triumphs over virtue. Pereda's masterpiece is generally considered to be *Sotileza* (1885), a sort of prose epic of the city of Santander and its inhabitants, high and low. The descriptions are excellent, the characters vital and impressive. The account of the storm at sea, in which one of the heroine Sotileza's three suitors is carried to death, is one of the best of its kind to be found anywhere. The scene of *Peñas arriba* (1893) is a remote mountain village presided over by Don Celso, who incarnates all the noble patriarchal virtues so dear to the author. The mode of life is described in great detail and with admirable vigor and picturesqueness. Pereda does not belong to the sweetness and light school, and he can present evil along with good, but he obviously is saying that Spain should be run by the benevolent lord of the manor, who will wisely guide the destinies of the contented tenantry. If Pereda's ideas are hopelessly outdated in a modern world, everyone must admire his sturdy sincerity and his vigorous literary artistry. Many regard him as the very best of Spain's regional novelists.

The virile **Doña Emilia Pardo Bazán,** Countess of Pardo Bazán (1852-1921), is thought of as the chief proponent of naturalism in the novel, and she specifically championed it in a rather polemical work called *La cuestión palpitante* (1883). She really approves of the naturalistic method of Zola and his compeers, but she does not share any belief in scientific, physiological determinism.

Pardo Bazán was a native of Galicia, and she described her region in many novels and short stories with accuracy, picturesqueness, and loving zest. No one can fail to read her who wants to know about Spain's rain-soaked northwest corner. She wrote voluminously, but her first works were unimpressive. Apart from short stories such as the excellent *Insolación* (1889) and *Morriña* (1889) (a Galician word meaning "homesickness"), her masterpiece is *Los pazos* ("manor-house") *de Ulloa* (1886) and its sequel *La madre naturaleza* (1887). The author was not good at structure, and the plot rambles considerably. The second title is ironical: kind Mother Nature in this case is the wicked stepmother who brings hero and heroine to incest. Some of the descriptions might suggest gutter realism, because Pardo Bazán shows no maidenly shrinking from ugliness, but the descriptions of Galician life show keen observation and sympathy and often have poetic beauty. The forty-three volumes of the Countess' *Obras completas* contain many more novels, short stories, literary studies, criticism and polemics, biographies and travel books. They are little read today.

Leopoldo Alas ("Clarín," 1852-1901) was a law professor and a critic who wrote some good prose fiction. He was liberal, keen, and often pugnacious. His region was Asturias, notably the city of Oviedo where he taught, and that city appears under the name of Vetusta in his long naturalistic novel called *La regenta* (*The Judge's Wife*) (1884-1885). The characters, high and low, notably the cathedral priests, are skillfully drawn, and the epic of the traditional old town is well narrated. Alas became a little less antitraditional in his later and less well-realized novels.

Armando Palacio Valdés (1853-1938) was a native of Asturias, and that region formed the background of some of his better novels. He really began with *El señorito Octavio* (1881), a contrast of real life with fiction, followed two years later by what many consider his best novel, *Marta y María*. The background is a small town in Asturias, and the Martha and Mary types are interestingly contrasted. *El idilio de un enfermo* (1884) is also Asturian. *José* (1885), one of the author's better-known works, is a novel of fishing life. *Riverita* (1886) and its second part, *Maximina* (1887), have their scene laid in Madrid. They contain delicate feminine portraits, in which the author excelled, are rather pessimistic in tone, and contain many autobiographical elements.

Extremely popular among Palacio's numerous novels is *La hermana San Sulpicio* (1889), a most interesting picture of Seville as seen through the eyes of an Asturian. It presents the Andalusia dreamed of by foreigners, with all its warm picturesqueness, and makes one long to visit or revisit the chief city of southern Spain. The author has the viewpoint of a tourist, and is not concerned with Andalusia's burning economic and social problems. *Los majos de Cádiz* (1896) goes even farther south for its background. Valencian customs are depicted in *La alegría del capitán Ribot* (1899). Among his works the author preferred *Tristán o el pesimismo* (1906), the story of a man who comes to grief because of his negative attitude toward humanity. *La novela de un novelista* (1921), its posthumous second part *Album de un ciego* (1940), and *Testamento literario* (1929) contain Palacio Valdés' autobiography and opinions on life and letters.

The works of Palacio are smoothly written, interestingly conceived, and easily read. Up to this century he was the Spanish author most translated after Cervantes.

Benito Pérez Galdós (1843-1920) was born in the Canary Islands but studied and spent the major portion of his life in Madrid. He also traveled all over Spain, and knew it as no one else did. Few would question his right to be called the greatest novelist of modern Spain. Even his fecundity was impressive: 46 volumes of historical *Episodios Nacionales,* 34 "social" novels in 42 volumes, 24 plays, 15 volumes of miscellaneous works.

His merits are, however, far more than quantitative, though he never received the Nobel Prize accorded to lesser Spaniards and to others. He came to Madrid ostensibly to study law, which all Spaniards seem to pursue in any case of doubt, but quickly gave it up for literature. He worked on a number of dramas never acted or published, but began his real literary career with a historical novel of the nineteenth century, always to be his field: *La fontana de oro* (1870), followed shortly by *El audaz.* He conceived the idea of writing a sort of fictionized history of Spain from 1808 onward, in which the imaginary characters would move among actual historical events, and in 1873 he began the first of the five series of the

Episodios Nacionales with *Trafalgar,* and the last, *Cánovas,* brings Spanish history down to the Restoration of 1874. The first two series of *Episodios,* published 1873-1875 and 1875-1879, are undoubtedly superior to the last three. Nothing could be more different from the "historical" novels à la Walter Scott than these realistic works of Galdós. Instead of being a falsely glamorized and little understood Middle Ages, the scene is near-contemporary, and the author got no little information from survivors of the events which he so vividly described. Galdós sought to give the spirit of the times, the motivating forces, the atmosphere, the spiritual climate, the private as well as the public activities of historical personages involved. By thus recounting their immediate past, he made Spaniards see themselves, often for the first time. No one who wishes to become acquainted with nineteenth-century Spain can afford to neglect the *Episodios.*

The creative power of Galdós is better shown in the remarkable number of his novels dissecting contemporary Spanish society, especially the middle classes. In *Doña Perfecta* (1876) he etches a somber picture of the results of religious fanaticism in an incurably traditional small Spanish cathedral city. Doña Perfecta finally orders the murder of her nephew because she is persuaded he represents vicious modern ideas. *Gloria* (1877) portrays the tragic career of a girl from a highly conservative family (her uncle is a bishop) who falls in love with an English Jew. Human happiness is wrecked on the reef of traditional ideas on both sides. *La familia de León Roch* (1879) is another thesis novel. Wife and husband become estranged because the wife is dominated by her confessor. It might be more accurate to say that León and his wife had merely ceased to love one another. *Marianela* (1878) is a pathetic idyll with its setting in the mining region of the north. It displays Galdós' constant sympathy for the weak and the unfortunate. *La desheredada* (1881), *Lo prohibido* (1884), and *Tormento* (1884) are rather naturalistic and most vivid pictures of the middle and lower classes of the Madrid which Galdós knew so remarkably well.

The long four-volume *Fortunata y Jacinta* (1886-1887) is generally considered Galdós' masterpiece. The scene is Madrid, and the characters of the two married women involved and their interactions are studied with analytical minuteness and great success. The canvas is very large, but all portions of it are carefully painted. The four novels of the *Torquemada* series (1889-1895) mainly show the effects of avarice on character. *Nazarín* (1895) describes a sort of modern Christ, and, along with *Halma* (1895), shows the influence of Tolstoy.

The last great novel of Galdós is *Misericordia* (1897). The characterization of the beggar Benigna, of the run-down family whom she serves, and of the blind Moorish beggar Almudena is masterly. The novel ends with the words of Benigna to her ungrateful mistress: "Go and sin no more."

Galdós constantly championed modern progress, and he was always a liberal, though not with starry eyes, and his effect on his country has been great. His literary style is not free from serious defects.

Vicente Blasco Ibáñez (1867-1928) achieved his celebrity in this century, but in spirit and method he belongs to Zolaesque naturalism. He has been called, not without justification, "a gifted vulgarian" and "a literary athlete." He is par excellence the novelist of the region of his native Valencia, which he admirably portrays in his earliest and best novels. *La barraca* (1898) is a somber and vivid picture of the peasant tenant farmers of the Valencian countryside. *Cañas y barro* (1902) has its scene laid in the rice-growing lagoons of the east, and spares the reader no tragic or sordid detail of the hard life there, including greed, lust, seduction, and infanticide. It is at least impressive. Blasco later devoted novels to various other parts of Spain, often propagandizing for advanced social or political ideas. *La catedral* (1903), anti-clerical, describes Toledo: *El intruso* (1904), Bilbao; *La bodega* (1905), on the evils of drink, Jerez; *Los muertos mandan* (1909), the Island of Ibiza, in the Balearics. *Sangre y arena* (1908), very familiar to movie-goers as *Blood and Sand,* is an admirable novel of bullfighting.

Blasco Ibáñez won international fame and wealth with his novel of the First World War, *Los cuatro jinetes del Apocalipsis* (1916). In it his vigor and great reportorial gifts are at their best. His later novels may be neglected without loss. He died in exile from the Spain of Alfonso XIII, because of his vigorous championing of a Spanish republic, which he did not live to see.

Blasco's literary style is forceful, energetic, and turbulent like the man himself. The word delicacy was not in his lexicon. Some of his short stories are excellent.

VERSE

The heading "verse" is used because of real poetry in the later nineteenth century there was a serious dearth.

Ramón de Campoamor (1817-1901) was a great celebrity in his day whose glory has now departed. He began writing romantic verse (he was born the same year as Zorrilla), but turned to seeking "art for the sake of the idea." His later verse tends to be rather skeptical, ironic, a sort of critique of romanticism. Campoamor thought of himself as a considerable philosopher, and wrote critical works. He invented terms for three groups of his poems. The *"doloras"* he fancily described as a sort of transcendental fable in which eternal verities are represented, and the *doloras* are usually short, mildly ironical, rather delicate, and a bit didactic. One particularly has survived: *¡Quién supiera escribir! (If I only knew how to write!),* in which an illiterate girl grieves because her priest-amanuensis will not let her write to her absent lover her simple expressions of affection. Campoamor's very brief *humoradas* are really epigrams, some not badly expressed. His *pequeños poemas* are longer, but share the same qualities.

Gaspar Núñez de Arce (1832-1903) had greater intrinsic gifts than Campoamor, but his tone is usually too loud and his diction is likely to be oratorical. He produced a few well-achieved and pathetic tales in verse, but his most characteristic volume is called *Gritos del combate* (1873). He shouts of the difficulties and disillusionments of life, including the conflict of faith and reason.

There were numerous other versifiers in the period, but they achieved no great reputation, not even in their own day, and are now just about forgotten.

THE DRAMA

Some of the romantic dramatists who began in the eighteen-thirties continued to produce well after mid-century. Younger playwrights made their bow to realism mainly by transferring their scenes from the Middle Ages to the present without greatly changing their attitudes. The general style continued mainly to be sentimental and high-sounding.

Manuel Tamayo y Baus (1829-1881), the son of a famous

actress, began by writing romantic plays and historical dramas, plus a classic tragedy, *Virginia* (1853). *La bola de nieve* (1856) shows the evils of jealousy, and the scene is contemporary. *Lo positivo* (1862) shows how the love of money is a root of all evil. *Lances de honor* (1863) condemns the duel. Tamayo's most famous play is on Shakespeare's Yorick, and is called *Un drama nuevo* (1867), a fine example of the play within a play. Alas, poor Yorick's young wife makes him jealous, and in the new drama they are putting on he really and truly stabs her lover, as the lines call for. The emotion is intense, or is meant to be, and the actors must scream or sob their lines in the best melodramatic tradition. Tamayo had an excellent knowledge of stagecraft.

Adelardo López de Ayala (1828-1878) also treats moral themes like Tamayo, and is a better versifier. He began before he was twenty-one with *Un hombre de estado* (historical; on the theme of Don Rodrigo Calderón), and produced numerous plays, including *zarzuelas* (musical comedies). Many dramatists of the time wrote them. In *El tanto por ciento* (1861) love finally triumphs over money-seeking. *Consuelo* (1863) shows how a vain and greedy woman who prefers luxury to true love receives condign punishment. *El nuevo don Juan* (1863) shows the new Don Juan as far more ridiculous than the injured husband. López de Ayala at least helped to relieve the Spanish drama from its dominant mediocrity.

José Echegaray (1832-1916) was a mathematics professor turned statesman turned dramatist, and he made more loud noises on the stage than anyone in his time. They were heard all the way to Sweden, and he was granted the Nobel Prize for Literature in 1904. His dramas, some in prose and some in verse, show his innate romanticism, and his characters tear their passion into fine shreds. His situations are forced and implausible. *O locura o santidad* (1877): the theme is that a man who is superhonorable will be considered mad by family and friends. Echegaray's most celebrated play, still occasionally put on today, is *El gran Galeoto* (1881). The idea is that slander may drive even honorable people to exaggerated misbehavior. More than one character swoons on the stage. *El hijo de don Juan* (1892) is an inferior rehash of Ibsen's *Ghosts*. The hero is forced to renounce marriage, glory, and all happiness, and dies screaming for the sun, as in Ibsen.

Echegaray's bombastic rhetoric now produces an impression of positive grotesqueness.

Many other minor dramatists thronged on the later nineteenth-century stage. It is more than possible that the unpretentious and still popular *zarzuelas* have the best chance of survival.

Joaquín Dicenta (1863-1917) is credited with bringing the proletariat to the Spanish stage, and his plays attack social injustice. *Juan José* (1895) shows an honest workman turned into a murderer because of the oppressions of an evil boss. Other plays which gave him a reputation are *Daniel* (1907), *El lobo* (1913). In the latter a callous criminal is romantically transformed by love. Dicenta, no dramatic genius, was at least realistic in the dialogue of his personages.

In the eighteen-nineties **Galdós** began dramatizing for stage presentation some of his already dramatic novels. The first was *Realidad* (1892), and the very title is significant. His plays, not all successful on the boards, treated social themes in a realistic manner, and were a sign of progress from the exaggerated thrillers of Echegaray. Galdós' most sensational play was *Electra* (1901), on the theme of the conflict between traditional fanaticism and modern rational attitudes. Galdós was excoriated in conservative quarters because his villain is a Jesuit priest. *El abuelo* (1904) shows that true worth and not blue blood constitutes real aristocracy. The play is not without exaggerated histrionics. *La de San Quintín* (1894) shows ruined aristocrats regenerated by useful employment, and the infusion of vigorous near-peasant blood. Galdós always exalted the self-made man. He performed a real service in bringing the stage to realistic sanity.

ORATORY, HISTORY, SCHOLARSHIP

A vast amount of Spanish literature has (since the importation of tobacco) gone up in smoke over café tables. More careful Spaniards saved their golden words for the pulpit or the tribune, and oratory has flourished vigorously at all periods, including the politically troubled nineteenth century.

Emilio Castelar (1832-1899), fertile as a writer, and liberal politician, was a famous orator. He was president of the short-lived First Spanish Republic in 1873. His rotund and rolling periods greatly impressed his contemporaries, including the American Ambassador John Hay. **Joaquín Costa** (1846-1911), predecessor of the Generation of 1898, had more effect through his speeches than through his writings.

Modesto Lafuente (1806-1866) published a vast *Historia de España* (1850-1857), in thirty volumes. It does not satisfy the demands of modern scholarship. **José Amador de los Ríos** (1818-1878) devoted himself, more critically and thoroughly, to medieval studies. He is particularly noted for his still most useful *Historia crítica de la literatura española* (1861-1865), in seven volumes. It reaches to the times of Ferdinand and Isabella.

Martín Fernández de Navarrete (1765-1844) wrote the first real biography of Cervantes, the *Vida de Miguel de Cervantes Saavedra* (1819). He also wrote a history of exploration in the New World.

Diego Clemencín (1765-1834) was the first great commentator on *Don Quixote*. **Pascual de Gayangos** (1809-1897) uncritically published many older Spanish texts, especially among the seventy volume *Biblioteca de Autores Españoles.* (plus one of Indexes), originally begun in 1846 and concluded in 1880. More volumes have been added in recent years. Gayangos rendered valuable service by translating George Ticknor's *History of Spanish Literature.*

Manuel Milá y Fontanals (1818-1884) was a much sounder scholar than Gayangos, and he particularly investigated the origins of the Castilian and Catalan epic and ballad.

Marcelino Menéndez y Pelayo (1856-1912) was endowed with a prodigious memory and phenomenal industry, and his scholarly and critical investigations touched almost every phase of Spanish literature and thought. When he was made Director of the National Library, it was said that he did not direct it, he read it. A list of some of his more important works will suggest the vastness of his achievement. New editions of his works have been made in recent years. *La ciencia española* (1876); *Horacio en España* (1877); *Historia de los heterodoxos españoles* (1880-1882); *Calderón y su teatro* (1881); *Historia de las ideas estéticas en España* (1883-1889, 9 vols.); *Obras dramáticas de Lope de Vega* (Spanish Academy ed., 13 vols., 1890-1902. Texts uncritical, introductions extensive); *Estudios de crítica literaria* (1884 onward); *Antología de poetas líricos castellanos* (1890-1908, 13 vols.);

Orígenes de la novela (1905-1910. 3 vols. of studies plus texts). Menéndez y Pelayo's patriotic and religious preoccupations limit the universality of his point of view, and there are errors of detail in his vast work, but his achievements were quite extraordinary. He was the teacher and inspirer of many scholars who followed him. Some of his contemporaries also made useful contributions to scholarship.

The Generation of 1898

THINKERS, ESSAY-ISTS, CRITICS	HISTORIANS AND SCHOLARS	NOVELISTS	DRAMATISTS	POETS
Forerunners:	Rafael Altamira (1866-1951)	Pío Baroja (1872-1956)	Jacinto Benavente (1866-1954)	Chief Precursor:
Angel Ganivet, (1865-1898)	Antonio Ballesteros, (1880-1949)	Ramón María del Valle-Inclán (1896-1936)	Gregorio Martínez Sierra (1881-1948)	Rubén Darío (1867-1916)
Joaquín Costa, (1846-1911)	Ramón Menéndez Pidal (1869—)	Gabriel Miró (1879-1930)	Manuel Linares Rivas (1867-1944)	Eduardo Marquina (1879-1946)
	Emilio Cotarelo (1858-1936)	Traditionalists:	Serafín (1871-1938) and Joaquín (1873-1944) Alvarez Quintero	Francisco Vallaespesa (1877-1935)
Miguel de Unamuno, (1864-1936)	Adolfo Bonilla (1875-1926)	Ricardo León (1877-1943)	Jacinto Grau (1877-1958)	Emilio Carrere (1880-1947)
Ramiro de Maeztu (1874-1936)		Concha Espina (1877-1955)	One-act Plays:	Manuel Machado (1874-1947)
Jose Martínez Ruiz ("Azorín"), (1874)			Carlos Arniches (1866-1943)	Antonio Machado (1875-1939)
			Pedro Muñoz Seca (1881-1936)	Juan Ramón Jiménez (1881-1956)
				J. M. Gabriel y Galán (1870-1905)
				V. Medina (1866-1936)

CHAPTER 11

The Generation of 1898

King: Alfonso XIII (1902-1931)

Alfonso XIII was in his teens at the time of Spain's defeat in the Spanish-American War. He and his advisers were not able to cope with Spain's problems, but the country profited by remaining neutral in World War I. General Primo de Rivera was accepted as dictator in 1923, after Spain had suffered further military disasters in Morocco. Municipal elections proved the unpopularity of the king's regime, and he hurriedly went into exile in 1931, and the Second Spanish Republic was proclaimed.

In addition to the histories of literature, especially Del Río, good books for reference are:

Laín Entralgo, Pedro, *La generación del noventa y ocho*. Madrid, 1945.

Torrente Ballester, Gonzalo, *Panorama de la literatura española contemporánea*. Madrid, 1956. Also contains an anthology and good bibliographical notes. 2d ed., 2 vols., 1961.

It is probable that the years from 1898 to the present have produced more solid artistic achievement than any comparable period of Spanish literature since the Golden Age. The nineteenth century shines mainly for one author, Galdós.

The soul-searching of the later years of the century preceding this one resulted in a pessimistic attitude on the part of Spaniards, who sought to explain to themselves why Spain had fallen from her former splendor. They constantly meditated on the "Problema de España," but in general lacked the power to act. Spain's defeat by the United States in 1898 came as a final shock. She had lost her American colonies in the early part of the nineteenth century, and now even Cuba, Puerto Rico, and the Philippines were wrested from her. Spain's internal political and economic problems were far from solution.

Writers who came to maturity at the close of the last century are commonly said to form the "Generation of 1898," even though some denied the existence of any such group, and those said to compose it differed markedly one from another in thought, in artistic ideals, and in procedures. At least they all protested in one way or another against what had gone just before, which they considered "lo viejo" ("old stuff"). They were against high-flown rhetoric, against exaggerated histrionics in the drama, against the emphatic tone in poetry, against sheer traditionalism in the novel. A favorite word with them was "regeneration," and many said it was high time that Spain should be "Europeanized." They did indeed become more conscious of intellectual and artistic currents in the rest of the world, and the effect was most salutary. Even if many were negativistic in their vital attitudes, they were able to create, and their artistic legacy is noteworthy. Their greatest achievement is probably in lyric poetry, but other genres to which they contributed are far from negligible. The Nobel Prize jury selected the poet Juan Ramón Jiménez in 1956. They had accorded the same honor to the dramatist Jacinto Benavente in 1922.

PRECURSORS

The great services of the novelist Pérez Galdós in revealing Spain to Spaniards themselves can hardly be overestimated. He was not blind to Spanish virtues, but he never failed to point out in his voluminous novels the blind traditionalism, the religious fanaticism, the aristocratic vacuity, the social sores, the political corruption observable in his nation. The young learned from him, as they did also from the naturalistic Clarín (Leopoldo Alas). Clarín died in 1901, but Galdós lived until 1920 and was personally known to most of the young men who were getting their start in literature.

Joaquín Costa (1846-1911) was not a successful politician, but in his writings and even more in his speeches he was constantly preoccupied with Spain's problems. His influence on younger men was considerable.

Angel Ganivet García (1865-1898) was a gifted, sensitive, and thoughtful native of Granada whose short life ended in madness and suicide. He wrote about his native city in *Granada la Bella* (1896), but his most important work was his *Idearium español* (1897). In it he meditates on the Spanish character, and suggests remedies for the evils he sees in his nation. In his *Conquista del reino de Maya por el último conquistador español Pío Cid* (1897), he ironically contrasts Spanish and European civilization with that of a tribe in Central Africa, and suggests that Spaniards were great conquerors, but unable to administer and hold their conquests. Another novel, *Los trabajos del infatigable creador Pío Cid* (1898), has descriptive and autobiographical elements, but is also a criticism of contemporary Spanish character and customs. Ganivet's ideas entered importantly into the spiritual formation of the men of the generation which immediately followed.

ESSAYISTS AND CRITICS

Miguel de Unamuno (1864-1936) was a sturdy Basque, born in Bilbao. He became professor of Greek and later rector of the old University of Salamanca, but spent much time in Madrid. A writer and talker of great earnestness and force, he was always likely to be in the opposition, and he made enemies, but had still more friends and disciples. He was fundamentally a thinker, though not a systematic philosopher, and his essays on all sorts of subjects were published in many volumes. His most admired work at home, and in translation abroad, was probably his *Del sentimiento trágico de la vida* (1913), in which he discusses with almost agonizing intensity the conflict between man's longing for immortality and his reason, which tells him no. Unamuno's novels, in which the characters are likely to be abstractions with human names, are so different from the usual run that the author called them not *novelas* but *nivolas*. Some of them are: *Paz en la guerra* (1897), *Amor y pedagogía* (1902), *Niebla* (1914), *Abel Sánchez* (1917). Volumes of short stories, which are excellent, are *El espejo de la muerte* (1913) and *Tres novelas ejemplares y un prólogo* (1920). The tercentenary *Vida de don Quijote y Sancho, según Cervantes* (1905) is a most sprightly commentary on Spain's literary masterpiece. Unamuno was not a successful dramatist, but his verse is noteworthy, never for beautiful or harmonious form, but for deep feeling and thought: *Poesías* (1907), *Rosario de sonetos líricos* (1911), *El Cristo de Velázquez* (1920), *Romancero del destierro* (1928, when Unamuno had been banished by the Primo de Rivera dictatorship). Unamuno was unquestionably one of the striking personalities of this century. Whether he will impress future critics as he did many of his contemporaries remains to be seen.

Ramiro de Maeztu (1874-1936), of Basque and English parentage, was thought of as one of "The Three" (Maeztu, Baroja, and Azorín) who rebelled most violently against the preceding generation. Maeztu devoted himself mainly to journalism, and in his later years became a militant Catholic, monarchist, and conservative. He was killed in the disturbances of 1936. For literature, his most stimulating book was composed of essays on *Don Quijote, Don Juan y la Celestina* (1926).

José Martínez Ruiz (Azorín) (1874-   ) was the foremost critic within the Generation of 1898, and the chief interpreter of the spirit of Castile. Apart from relatively brief participation in politics (he was five times *Diputado a Cortes* between 1907 and 1919) his long life has been devoted to writing, with articles and books appearing every year. His style is antirhetorical and quiet, and he achieved a remarkable distillation of "the poetry of the commonplace." His knowledge of Spain and Spanish literature was vast, and his interpretations always revealed some new or unsuspected aspect. His complete works are still in course of publication. Important among them are: *El alma castellana, 1600-1800* (1900), *La voluntad* (1902; it was indeed will power for action that the generation lacked), *Antonio Azorín* (1903), *Las confesiones de un pequeño filósofo* (1904), *España* (1909), *Castilla* (1912), *El paisaje de España visto por los españoles* (1917), *Una hora de España* (1924); then a series of not too successful dramas and surrealistic works; *Pensando en España* (1940), *Memorias inmemoriales* (1946).

HISTORIANS AND SCHOLARS

Rafael Altamira (1866-1951) wrote on Spanish history, not as a succession of dynasties and battles but as an evolution of political, social, and cultural changes, with a liberal attitude on the part of the author. Best known is his *Historia de España y de la civilización española* (5 vols, in 6, Barcelona 1900-1930). An excellent one-volume work (in English) is his *History of Spain* (1949).

Antonio Ballesteros (1880-1949) was the author of an

extensive *Historia de España y su influencia en la historia universal* (9 vols. in 10,) 1918-1941, which may always be consulted with profit.

Ramón Menéndez Pidal (1869-   ) has long been internationally recognized as the dean of Spanish scholars, and a mere list of his valuable publications would fill many pages. He has been fundamentally a medievalist, but he has enriched the study of many phases of Spanish literature, language, and history, and he has been the teacher and master of the foremost linguistic and literary scholars of two generations. He has received the highest honors at home and abroad, and is everywhere regarded as one of the most distinguished scholarly investigators in the world. His first important study was *La leyenda de los Infantes de Lara* (1896). His *Manual de gramática histórica española* appeared first in 1904, and has been many times improved and reprinted. His masterly edition of the *Cantar de Mío Cid* (3 vols., 1908-1912) consolidated his reputation among scholars. In 1914 he founded the indispensable *Revista de Filología Española*. In 1924 appeared his *Poesía juglaresca y juglares,* now in its sixth edition. His *Orígenes del español* (1926) is a masterpiece in the study of Romance linguistics. *La España del Cid* appeared in 1929. He has written many studies of Spanish epic, lyric, and ballad poetry. He has directed the great *Historia de España,* still in course of publication with the collaboration of many specialists.

Emilio Cotarelo y Mori (1858-1936), even older than Menéndez Pidal, devoted himself especially to studies and editions of Spanish dramatists of the Golden Age and the eighteenth century. He edited three volumes of the plays of Tirso de Molina and ten of those of Lope de Vega, two volumes of *Entremeses,* and the *Sainetes* of Ramón de la Cruz.

Adolfo Bonilla y San Martín (1875-1926), disciple of Menéndez y Pelayo, devoted himself to studies of philosophy and literature. His editions of various texts (books of chivalry, picaresque novels, and especially of the complete works of Cervantes, in collaboration with the American Hispanist Rudolph Schevill) are still standard. Perhaps his most noteworthy study is that of *Luis Vives y la filosofía del Renacimiento* (1903).

NOVELISTS

Pío Baroja (1872-1956) was the most antiacademic, frank, sincere, and original Spanish novelist of the first half of this century. He was also one of the most fertile, since his works number around one hundred. He was one of several Spanish doctors who turned from medicine to literature, and his factual and usually skeptical observations of Spanish life have sometimes the odor of the clinic, though not the technique of Zola and the French naturalists. His favorite philosophers were Nietzsche and Schopenhauer, his favorite literary models Poe, Dickens, Balzac, Stendhal, and Dostoyevsky. His view of life and of human character was pessimistic, and he expressed his opposition to accepted values—army, church, state, pedagogical methods, just about everything—with great vigor and sincerity. His rugged style often seems unkempt, though he said his ideal was to achieve "rhetoric in a minor key." His sentences and paragraphs are usually short, and he bothers very little about well-knit plots. His novels seem rather a series of fragments, but there is an air of freshness in his direct and spontaneous vision of people and things. A few of his more important novels are: *Camino de perfección* (1902), *El Mayorazgo de Labraz* (1903), a trilogy on the poor in Madrid called *La lucha por la vida* (1904), *Paradox, rey* (1906), *Zalacaín el aventurero* (1909), *El árbol de la ciencia* (1911), *César o nada* (1912), a long series of novels under the general title *Memorias de un hombre de acción,* such as *El caballero de Erláiz* (1943). Baroja's long *Memorias* were published in 1955.

Ramón María del Valle-Inclán (1866-1936) is the opposite of Baroja in practically every respect, for he constantly sought aristocratic delicacy in his bejeweled poetry or prose. He was a literary exquisite who used all sensations for artistic purposes, constantly seeking beauty in cadenced and melodious sentences. His verse in general followed the pattern of Rubén Darío, and his plays, not very successful on the stage, contain much more poetry than dramatic intensity. He lives mainly through his novels, of which the best known are the four *Sonatas,* one for each season, in the love life of the Marqués de Bradomín, a modern Don Juan who was "ugly, a Catholic, and a sentimentalist." They were published from 1902 to

1905. *Flor de santidad* (1904) retells a legend set in the author's native rustic Galicia. A trilogy on the Carlist war, *Los cruzados de la causa, El resplandor de la hoguera* and *Gerifaltes de antaño,* with scenes of barbaric cruelty, appeared in 1908-9. Some of his later works Valle-Inclán called *esperpentos,* combinations of the poetic, the popular, the realistic, and the grotesque, always satirical. *Tirano Banderas* (1926) is a sanguinary satire of a Mexican dictator. The novels of the series called *El Ruedo Ibérico,* which might almost be called grotesqueries, employ popular as well as stylized language, and are a bitter satire of the stuffed-shirt politicians and their activities in the second half of the nineteenth century. Valle-Inclán also wrote numerous short stories. By many the author is regarded as the most artistic prose stylist of his generation.

Gabriel Miró (1879-1930) had a hard struggle with the economic realities of life, but never relinquished his artistic ideals in his numerous novels and short stories. He is a master of evocation, and his style may suggest a combination of Azorín and Valle-Inclán. He excels in description rather than narration. One may mention especially *La novela de mi amigo* (1908), *La cerezas del cementerio* (1910), *Figuras de la pasión del Señor* (1916), *El humo dormido* (1919), *Nuestro padre San Daniel* (1921), *El obispo leproso* (1925), and *Años y leguas* (1928).

Ricardo León (1877-1943) had no connection whatever with the Generation of 1898, whose attitudes he contemned. He progressed from banking into literature, but his conservatism remained undiminished. To most, his overblown style, based on servile imitation of Spanish classics, is likely to seem as old-fashioned as his traditional ideas. He possessed some insight into human behavior and considerable vigor, and his works were quite popular. Some novels: *Casta de hidalgos* (1908), *Alcalá de los Zegríes* (1909), *El amor de los amores* (1910), *Amor de caridad* (1922), *Los trabajadores de la muerte* (1927), *Jauja* (1928), *Cristo en los infiernos* (1943).

Concha Espina (1877-1955) was not a major novelist, but her qualities as a person, her sentimentality, her good will, her realistic descriptions, and her rather careful style endeared her to many readers. Among her numerous novels may be mentioned: *La niña de Luzmela* (1909), *La esfinge maragata*

(1913), *El metal de los muertos* (1921), *Altar mayor* (1926), *Retaguardia* (1937), and *Una novela de amor* (1953).

DRAMATISTS

Jacinto Benavente (1866-1954) once said that he had buried four generations of adverse critics, and he was about right. He began producing plays in 1894 (*El nido ajeno*), and in 1922 he was awarded the Nobel Prize for Literature. He continued to produce up to the time of his death. His theater is generally quietly satirical, a sort of protest against the screaming style of Echegaray. His plays read about as well as they play. His characters are typically of the upper and well-off bourgeoisie of Madrid, the very people who enjoyed seeing themselves, or at least their neighbors, satirized on the stage. The tone is sophisticated and mildly ironical, and the scene is likely to be a well-furnished drawing room. There are exceptions: *La malquerida* (1913, and many Americans saw it under the title *The Passion Flower*) is a pretty grim tragedy in a rustic setting, using popular dialect, and belies the accusation that Benavente wrote only plays without action and without passion. His technique is skillful and his dialogue clever and urbane. Probably his most famous play is *Los intereses creados* (1907), a modern comedy in the language and dress of a puppet show. Other plays well worthy of mention are: *Gente conocida* (1896), *La comida de las fieras* (1898), *La noche del sábado* (1903), *Rosas de otoño* (1905), *Señora ama* (1908), *Pepa Doncel* (1928), *Aves y pájaros* (1940), *La infanzona* (1946). Benavente also wrote charming plays for children, for whom he had great sympathy, such as *El príncipe que todo lo aprendió en los libros* (1919).

Gregorio Martínez Sierra (1881-1948) wrote poems, novels, essays, newspaper and magazine articles, and translated various foreign plays, but he is mostly known for his own amusing, light, and often rather sentimental original plays, the fame of which finally landed him in Hollywood. In some plays one feels the influence of Maeterlinck, and perhaps the participation of his gifted wife, María de la O Lejárraga. His *El amor brujo* is universally known through ballet music of Falla. Among his successes were: *La sombra del padre* (1909), *El ama de la casa* (1910), *Canción de cuna* (1911, perhaps his most delicate and most famous play), *Primavera en otoño* (1911), *Mamá* (1912), *El reino de Dios* (1916), *Sueño de una noche de agosto* (1918), *Don Juan de España* (1921), *Triángulo* (1930).

Manuel Linares Rivas (1867-1938) was a lawyer turned dramatist who had more skill and wit than some critics are willing to grant him. His contemporaries esteemed him enough to make him deputy, judge, senator, and member of the Spanish Academy, and some of his plays were good popular successes. He often brought social and legal problems to the stage. In general matters he follows the lead of Benavente, and he shares the aspiration of the "Men of '98" to renovate Spain. He is most noted for: *El abolengo* (1940), *Lady Godiva* (1912), *Como buitres* (1913), *La garra* (favoring divorce, 1914), *La fuerza del mal* (1914), *Cobardías* (1919), *Cristobalón* (1920), *La mala ley* (1923), *Mal año de lobos* (1927), *Todo Madrid lo sabía*.

Eduardo Marquina (1879-1946) was born in Barcelona and died in New York, where he was on a diplomatic mission. He began as a modernist poet and turned to the verse drama, always with the same interest in Spanish national themes, which he presented with vigor and perhaps with excessive grandiosity. The titles of his plays often speak for themselves: *Las hijas del Cid* (1908), *Doña María la Brava* (1909), *En Flandes se ha puesto el sol* (1910, on the last days of Spain in the Low Countries, probably the author's best play), *Teresa de Jesús* (1933). He also wrote straight nonhistorical plays such as *Cuando florezcan los rosales* (1914).

Serafín (1871-1938) and **Joaquín** (1873-1944) **Alvarez Quintero** were constantly collaborating dramatists born south of Seville who never recovered from the spell of their native southern Andalusia. They had no great intellectuality or dramatic inventiveness, but they poured forth a steady stream of comedies which presented all the warmth, charm, grace, and wit commonly attributed to their region, with great success. They were not profound, but they were often screamingly funny, and the theater-going public preferred anyway not to think about the burning economic and social problems of southern Spain. Their theater may not survive, but it had appealing charm. They were only occasionally serious, as in *Los Galeotes* (1900, a study of ingratitude). Some of their dramatic pictures of Andalusian life, scenes, and character have a truly delicate charm, as in the early *El patio* and *Las flores* (both 1901). Among their many other plays are: *El amor que pasa* (1904), *El genio alegre* (1906), *Malvaloca* (1912), *Puebla de las mujeres* (1912), *Doña Clarines* (1909), *La boda de Quinita Flores* (1925).

The dramatist **Jacinto Grau** (1877-1959) always remained somewhat apart from his generation. For one thing, much of his life was spent outside Spain, though Spain was never absent from his thought. His was a theater for select minorities, as though he were scorning popular appeal, for his themes were elevated, his language aristocratic in tone, with little if any crisp dramatic dialogue. He was and is esteemed by a small élite. Among his plays may be mentioned: *Entre llamas* (1905), *El Conde Alarcos* (1917), *El señor de Pigmalión* (1927), *El burlador que no se burla* (1928).

The tradition of the one-act play has always been strong in Spain, from Lope de Rueda through Quiñones de Benavente, Ramón de la Cruz, to the Quinteros and others. Two who successfully cultivated the genre in the twentieth century were these:

Carlos Arniches (1866-1943) pleased two generations with his skits—*sainetes, farsas,* even full plays—mainly dealing with the picturesque aspects of life in the less economically favored quarters of Madrid. He had considerable verve and comic sense. He and other *madrileñistas* not only presented life as they saw it in the back streets, they also invented attractive slang and modes of behavior, so that the social underworld attending or reading their productions learned how picturesquely they should talk and act, and proceeded to do so.

Pedro Muñoz Seca (1881-1936), though born on the far southern coast of Spain, came to Madrid and furnished the not too discriminating public with a long series of little plays called *astracanadas*. The word applies to little stage pieces filled with puns, as ridiculous and cockeyed as their language and situations in general. He was a real master of his not too delicate dramatic art. His best play is a parody in verse of the tragedy in general, called *La venganza de don Mendo*. He gave his plays an anti-Republican turn after 1931, and he was killed in Madrid in the early months of the Civil War, in 1936.

LYRIC POETS

The renovation of lyric poetry in Spain after the last years of the nineteenth century was remarkable, and one is at a loss in trying to choose among the hosts of really worthy poets who have sprung up from then until now. The main impetus came from the Nicaraguan **Rubén Darío** (1867-1916) and his Latin-American congeners, who were greatly influenced by the French Parnassians and symbolists, notably Paul Verlaine. The influence was assimilated, and was not parrot-like imitation. One should mention the somewhat similar aspirations of the Spanish **Salvador Rueda,** (1857-1933) who began even earlier. Darío represents what is called *Modernismo,* a term applied to the aspiration toward formal beauty, toward poetic expression rather than intellectual content, a protest against both superexuberant romantic subjectivity and the depressingly prosaic quality of poets like Campoamor. Sculptural, pictorial, musical, sensuous beauty was the ideal. Dario's *Azul* (prose and verse) appeared in 1888. Obviously Spanish poetic genius merely awaited inspiration, and from the late nineteenth century onward no such lyric outpouring has been seen since the Golden Age. Darío himself became less French and more Spanish with the publication of his lovely *Prosas profanas* (1896) and *Cantos de vida y esperanza* (1905). Both volumes contain poems of extraordinary sensuousness and musicality, and mark a most successful effort toward the renovation of Spanish metrics.

Marquina and **Valle-Inclán,** perhaps more eminent in other literary genres, were among those who early felt the inspiring breath of modernism. **Francisco Villaespesa** (1877-1936), who led the life of the most exaggerated poet of Bohemia, also found in modernism an appropriate climate, and his poetry is all gorgeous imagery, melodious sound, and Oriental splendor, even if his true poetic inspiration was shallow and his expression fundamentally careless. He reminds one of José Zorrilla, making due allowance for the different epoch. Villaespesa was for a time even considered by a good many readers of poetry as the chief of the modernists.

Emilio Carrere (1880-1947) translated Verlaine into Spanish and was much influenced by him. The Spanish poet made himself the singer of the Bohemia of Madrid and of the dregs of society. He occasionally sings with a note of his own.

Manuel Machado (1874-1947) came from Seville. His Andalusianism is prominent in his poems, and he is the best of the Spanish poets who remained faithful, though with a personal note, to the general manner of Darío and the modernists. The grace, charm, humor, and sensuality of the Spanish south are conspicuous in his highly musical compositions, many of them *coplas, seguidillas (seguiriyas)*, and other Andalusian verse forms. He has also used Spanish historical figures for poetic presentation, as in his famous word portrait of King Philip IV. He never sins against elegance, and his poems make delightful reading. He and his brother Antonio wrote a number of verse dramas. A few volumes: *Alma* (1900), *Museo* (1910), *Cante hondo* (1912), *Sevilla y otros poemas* (1921), *Horas de oro* (1938), *Obras completas* (1940).

Antonio Machado (1875-1939) grew up with his brother Manuel in Seville and Madrid, but became a greater poet, with a very distinct personality. He too began as a disciple of Darío, about 1899, although he moved rapidly away from ornamentation and toward simplicity. He lived and worked as a translator with his brother Manuel for a time in Paris. The poems of his first period are well represented in *Soledades* (1903), and *Soledades, galerías y otros poemas* (1907). In 1907 he became professor of French in the old Castilian town of Soria, and the severe landscape and spirit of Castile captured him from then onward. In 1909 he married a girl of sixteen. They were most happy until she became ill, and died after their return to Soria, in 1912. Her loss made an ineradicable impression on the poet. Some of his best verse is from the period of Soria: *Campos de Castilla* (1912), in which his preoccupations are with love, with the landscape and spirit of Castile, and the historical atmosphere of Spain. Not being able to stand Soria, Machado transferred to Baeza, province of Jaén, in his native Andalusia, where he remained until 1919. In this third period he is less like a native of the south than like a Castilian who utilizes popular Andalusian themes. In 1919 he returned to Castile, to Segovia, where he taught and founded a highly esteemed People's University. In 1931 he was brought to Madrid. From 1917 on he published his poems, mainly *Poesías completas,* adding to them in successive editions. His *Nuevas canciones* appeared in 1925, his poems of the Civil War, *La guerra,* in 1937. His philosophical meditations, called *Juan de Mairena,* in prose, appeared that same year. The poems of his last period are more thoughtful than before, at times even epigrammatic. The plays of the two Machado brothers, all but one in verse, are mainly on historical themes, and do not equal their lyrics.

Antonio Machado was a fervent patriot who vigorously served the cause of the Second Republic. Forced to flee his country upon Franco's victory in January of 1939, sick in body and heart, he died, as did his aged mother, a few days later in the little French town of Collioure. Some think that his lyricism was the deepest of the Spain of his time.

Juan Ramón Jiménez (1881-1958) received the Nobel Prize for Literature in 1956, toward the end of a life consecrated with complete devotion to lyric poetry. He was born in the extreme south of Spain, at Moguer, but one finds very little real Andalusianism in his verse. His father was a Castilian anyway. In 1900 he came to Madrid, as he says "with deep spring melancholy." He had been for much of his life a semi-invalid and depressive, sustained and protected by his talented wife Zenobia Camprubí, who died in 1956. His life from 1900 to 1936 was spent mainly in Madrid, with time out for illness and for travel. As a result of the Civil War, he went to Puerto Rico in 1936, and afterwards to the United States, South America, and again to Puerto Rico, as one of many gifted exiles from Franco's Spain.

It may be that there have been better poets in twentieth century Spain than Juan Ramón (as he is usually called), but none with quite so much influence on younger poets. He himself began under the influence of Rubén Darío. In fact it was Darío who suggested the title of one of his first volumes, *Almas de violeta* (1900), and Valle-Inclán another (*Ninfeas;* the word means "water-lilies," 1900). Villaespesa was also his friend.

It was not long before Juan Ramón began to emancipate himself, to free his verse from accessories, to seek the ideal of absolute beauty to which he has constantly aspired, since to him poetry and life itself have always been one. He calls on his gods to give him the exact, naked essence of things, and his labor has been one of purification, as he says: "la depuración de lo mismo." He endeavors never to put in a single word that is not the irreplaceable one, and his poetry is constantly pruned and polished.

In 1917, the recently married Juan Ramón published not only his verse *Diario de un poeta recién casado,* but also his version, in highly imaginative and poetic prose, of his supposed wanderings with a donkey, entitled *Platero y yo,* twice translated into English and highly esteemed by savorers of esthetic delicacies.

Even the idolatrous admirers of Juan Ramón' Jiménez might admit that his fertility has been excessive, that there are many lines and whole poems that add little to his glory. As early as 1920 some critics suggested that he had best be read in an anthology. A good one is his own very large *Tercera antolojía poética* (1957), in which the essence of his achievement can be savored. A list of all his separate volumes would be far too long.

No one will seek in Juan Ramón robustness, virility, real scope, or the spontaneous lyric spirit of Lope or of the Elizabethans. If he is a minor poet among the world's greatest, his has none the less been a true poetic achievement.

Among regional poets, rather apart from their contemporaries, one might mention **José María Gabriel y Galán** (Castile and Estremadura; 1870-1905), and **Vicente Medina** (Murcia, 1866-1936).

Post-1898. 1925. Civil War to the Present

Post-1898. 1925. Civil War to the Present

THINKERS, ESSAYISTS AND SCHOLARS	NOVELISTS	DRAMATISTS	POETS
J. Ortega y Gasset (1883-1955)	R. Pérez de Ayala (1880–)	J. M. Pemán (1898–)	E. Díez-Canedo (1879-1944)
E. d'Ors (1883-1954)	R. Gómez de la Serna (1888–)	E. Jardiel Poncela (1901–)	León Felipe (1884–)
M. Azaña (1880-1940)	A. Barea (1897-1957)	J. Calvo Sotelo (1905–)	R. de Basterra (1887-1928)
G. Marañón (1887–)	R. Sender (1902–)	A. Casona (1903–)	J. Moreno Villa (1889-1904)
S. de Madariaga (1886–)	J. A. de Zunzunegui (1901–)	A. Buero Vallejo (1916–)	P. Salinas (1892-1951)
A. Castro (1885–)	C. J. Cela (1916–)	V. Ruiz Iriarte (1912–)	J. Guillén (1893–)
P. Laín Entralgo (1908–)	J. M. Gironella (1917–)	G. López Rubio (1903–)	G. Diego (1896–)
J. L. Aranguren (1909–)	C. Laforet (1921–)	A. Sastre (1926–)	D. Alonso (1898–)
J. Ferrater Mora (1909–)	E. Quiroga (1921–)	C. Muñiz	V. Aleixandre (1900–)
J. Marías (1914–)	M. Delibes (1920–)	A. Paso (1926–)	R. Alberti (1902–)
G. de Torre (1900–)	G. Goytisolo (1931–)		F. García Lorca (1898-1936)
X. Zubiri (1898–)	J. Agustí (1913–)		L. Cernuda (1904–)
	L. Romero (1916–)		L. Rosales (1910–)
	G. Suárez Carreño,		L. F. Vivanco (1907–)
	D. Fernández Flórez,		L. Panero (1909–)
	L. Romero (1916–)		J. Panero (1910–)
			M. Hernández (1910-1942)
			D. Ridruejo (1912–)
			C. Bousoño (1923–)

These lists might be greatly enlarged. Dates are taken mainly from the Bleiberg-Marías *Diccionario*, and the Torrente Ballester *Panorama*.

CHAPTER 12

Post-1898. 1925. Civil War to the Present

Alfonso XIII 1902-1931. 2nd Spanish Republic 1931-1939. Civil War 1936-1939. Franco Dictatorship 1939—.

Most Spanish intellectuals of all ages shared in the dissatisfaction with the management of affairs in the reign of Alfonso XIII and the establishment of the Republic in 1931 was hailed with high hopes in Spain and abroad. The constitution finally adopted was democratic and liberal. Unfortunately those in charge of the government proved inept, and for many reasons the republic was a failure. Conservatives of all stripes were dissatisfied, and finally Francisco Franco and other generals who had sworn allegiance to the republic rebelled in 1936, secured the aid of Hitler and Mussolini, and early in 1939 won a final victory, costing more than a million lives on the two sides. Spain remained neutral in World War II. Franco, called "Chief of State," has had no serious challenge to his dictatorship.

No good name has been found to characterize a group of authors who began their production after the Generation of 1898 had become reasonably well established. The term "Generation of 1925" is by no means precise. These younger men were in general products of more solid university training, they were already familiar with more general European cultural aspirations, and they could hardly be called imitators or disciples of their older companions. They might admire their elders, but they were sometimes in ideological and artistic opposition to them. One readily senses differences from ideals and procedures in vogue around 1900. It is not to be forgotten that certain authors of the Generations of 1898 continued to produce until well into the nineteen-fifties. Three generations thus overlap.

THINKERS, ESSAYISTS, AND SCHOLARS

José Ortega y Gasset (1883-1955) belies the often-made statement that Spain has produced no philosophers, because his influence as a thinker has been important not only in his own country but also in the rest of the world. Solidly trained in Spain and in Germany, he became professor of metaphysics in the University of Madrid, in 1910. In subsequent years he traveled and lectured widely in Europe and the Americas, and his very numerous writings gained wide circulation. His *Obras completas* (Madrid, 1946-1947) by no means contain all that he has written. In 1923 he founded Spain's most important modern journal, the *Revista de Occidente,* of happy memory.

Ortega speaks of life as a "radical reality," and of the individual as composed of the self and its "circumstance." He has given the world stimulating meditations not only on philosophy, but also on vital literary and artistic problems. A few of his important works are: *Meditaciones del Quijote* (1914), *España invertebrada* (1921), *El tema de nuestro tiempo* (1923), *La rebelión de las masas* (1930), of worldwide popularity and influence, *La deshumanización del arte* (1925), *Ideas y creencias* (1940).

Eugenio d'Ors (1883-1954) used the pen name of Xenius, and his essays and books including those on art criticism, enjoyed wide circulation. His first publications were in his native Catalan, his later ones in Castilian, in an original and highly polished style. He was best known for his *Glosario* (1906-1920). His philosophy is summarized in *El secreto de la filosofía* (1947).

Manuel Azaña (1880-1940) is thought of chiefly as an important political figure (Prime Minister, later President of the Republic, 1936), but he was also a novelist, essayist, dramatist, and literary critic of note. He is particularly known for excellent studies of Juan Valera.

Gregorio Marañón (1887-1960) belongs to the same generation. As a professor of endocrinology in the University of Madrid he has published internationally respected scientific works, but he has also published many others belonging to history and literature, such as his studies on Henry IV of

Castile, on Don Juan as a psychological and literary type, on Luis Vives, on the Count-Duke of Olivares, on El Greco, and on Antonio Pérez.

Salvador de Madariaga (1886-   ) has been journalist, diplomat, professor (Oxford), traveler, lecturer, historian, biographer, essayist and critic, and writes in an attractive style in Spanish, English, and French. He synthesizes the ideas regarding Spain of the Europeanizers, the Generation of 1898 and of Ortega y Gasset. Important among his works are his biographies of Columbus, Hernán Cortés, and Bolívar; *Ensayos angloespañoles* (1922), *España* (1931, reworked and revised in English and in Spanish, in later editions). *Guía del lector del "Quijote"* (1926).

Among the many noteworthy pupils of Menéndez Pidal is **Américo Castro** (b. 1885), who early achieved an international reputation for his philological and literary studies. He taught at the University of Madrid and in various foreign universities, notably Princeton, until his retirement. His *El pensamiento de Cervantes* (1925) marked an epoch in Cervantine studies. His *España en su historia: cristianos, moros y judíos* (1948), next published in English in 1954 and finally published with revisions and additions as *La realidad histórica de España* (Mexico, 1957) is a series of subtle and stimulating meditations of what has constituted the essence of Spain.

Xavier Zubiri (b. 1898) possesses a solid scientific and philosophic culture, acquired in Spain, Belgium, and Germany. His penetrating essays were collected and published in 1944 as *Naturaleza, Historia, Dios*. He gave up his professorship in the University of Madrid for private teaching and lecturing. His reputation seems to have grown steadily.

José Gaos (b. 1902) translated Heidegger and Husserl, and has continued his philosophical publications in exile in Mexico.

It would be an ungrateful and nearly impossible task even to list the numerous highly capable living Spanish scholars who have enriched various branches of Spanish learning. One should note also the contributions of numerous foreign Hispanists, in Europe and in the Americas, who have deserved well of the country of their predilection.

NOVELISTS

Ramón Pérez de Ayala (1880   ) was unquestionably the most intellectual novelist of his day, but he has a deep sense of reality and a fine and often ironic sense of humor. His style, in his poems, his criticism and his prose fiction, is extremely flexible. He can pass quickly from the philosophy of Plotinus or the hymns of the Breviary to charmingly bawdy jests. He was educated by the Jesuits, and turned violently against them in his ironically entitled novel *A.M.D.G.* (1910). *La pata de la raposa* (1911) and *Troteras y danzaderas* (1913) show young men struggling to cope with the complexities of modern society, and lost for their indecisiveness, their lack of will. The three *Novelas poemáticas* (1916) are remarkably intense. *Belarmino y Apolonio* (1921) tells the strange careers of a shoemaker-philosopher and a shoemaker-dramatist. In *Tigre Juan* and its sequel *El curandero de su honra* (both 1926), Ayala paints a more than life-size character who finally is cured of his great admiration for Calderonianism and Don Juanism. One must know Spanish backgrounds to appreciate the work, but it is a real achievement. Ayala's many admirers have greatly regretted that he produced no more novels.

The inexhaustible and purposely eccentric **Ramón Gómez de la Serna** (1888-   ) can sit down and dash off a book on any subject: circuses, the dead, bullfighters, breasts (a rather long book), Oscar Wilde, a white and black widow, and dozens more, and he can make them amusing and stimulating if not completely intelligible. His voluminous literary work defies classification. It might in general be described as a tremendous series of metaphors, in the creation of which he might rival Góngora or Quevedo. More accurately, RAMÓN, as he prefers to be called, states that his favorite form, the *greguería*, is humorous attitude plus metaphor, and it suggests new visions of everyday things. He has written several volumes entitled *Greguerías*, ever since 1910. His so-called novels, without sustained plots, can be as interesting as some of their titles: *El doctor inverosímil* (1922), *La malicia de las acacias*, *El torero Caracho* (1926), *Seis falsas novelas* (1926); one might call them antinovels), *Novelas superhistóricas*, etc., etc. He calls his autobiography *Automoribundia*.

He began publishing when he was sixteen, and never stopped. He lived in Argentina after the fall of the republic but later returned to Spain.

POSTMODERNISTIC POETS

Poets who arose after the time when Rubén Darío was the most important influence were no longer satisfied with marmoreal form, gorgeous suggestiveness, and lovely musicality. Statements even arose such as: "We must wring the neck of the swan." Poetry in Spain has since been vastly different from that of the modernists, though all sorts of tendencies have been manifest. Among earlier postmodernist poets one might mention **Enrique Díez-Canedo** (1879-1944), **León Felipe** (b. 1884), **Ramón de Basterra** (1887-1928) and **José Moreno Villa** (1889-1954).

Two professors of Spanish in the United States have been among the better poets of their time. **Pedro Salinas** (1892-1951) was teacher (Seville, Murcia, The Sorbonne, Cambridge, Madrid, Wellesley, Johns Hopkins), scholar, critic, and poet. His highly refined verses, usually not in formal patterns, deal mainly with love, but not in any romantically anguished or conventionally traced way. The expression is restrained, perhaps even intellectualized, yet one gets a sense of true emotion expressed in modern terms. Some works: *Presagios* (1923), *Seguro azar* (1929), *La voz a ti debida* (1934), *Razón de amor* (1936), *Poesía junta* (1942).

Jorge Guillén (1893-   ) taught at the Sorbonne, Murcia, Seville, Oxford, and from 1938 at Wellesley College. Many consider his verse the most classical of the moderns. His forms are usually conventional ones, though with modifications, and he has sought to produce a poetry free from accessories, a poetry more of things than of persons and commonplace feelings. His poems, like those of Salinas, are by no means for those who read only newspaper sports sections. He calls his major poetic work *Cántico,* enlarged in various editions. The fourth (1950) contains 334 poems. He has also translated Valéry, Supervielle, Claudel and Cassou. His last works have been *Maremágnum* (1957) and *Viviendo y otros poemas* (1958).

Dámaso Alonso (b. 1898) is a lyric poet who is also a highly trained literary investigator and critic, and who has taught in Germany, England, the United States, and is now professor at the University of Madrid. He has traveled and lectured widely in Europe and the New World. He has translated Shelley, James Joyce, and T. S. Eliot and has studied many phases of Spanish poetry, from the *jarchas* through *Poetas españoles contemporáneos* (1952). His original poems, usually irregular in form, are contained in such volumes as: *Poemas puros: Poemillas de la ciudad* (1921), *Oscura noticia* (1944), *Hijos de la ira* (1944), *Hombre y Dios* (1955). The poetry of Dámaso Alonso is characterized by deeply sincere emotion and thought, often with religious implications.

Gerardo Diego (b. 1896) is a professor, musician, critic of art and of literature, and a lyric poet of note. He is thought of as one of the most advanced vanguardist poets, but he has been attracted by classic forms and themes as well as by the most advanced modern tendencies, such as creationism: "To create what we shall never see, that is poetry." Diego has exerted considerable influence. Among his volumes may be mentioned: *Imagen* (1922), *Versos humanos* (1925), *Poemas adrede* (1943), *Amazona* (1955). Diego's *Fábula de Equis y Zeda,* published in Mexico, represents his more exaggerated and dehumanized verse.

Vicente Aleixandre (b. 1900), who stands rather apart in his generation, has said that the poet is both bard and prophet and that his poetry is "directed to that which is most permanent in man." His verse has been called a combination of romanticism and surrealism. He endeavors to express, preferably in long, free lines, what he calls the universally human. Quite popular in Spain, he has made little impression abroad. His rather personal *Historia del corazón* was published in 1954, after numerous other volumes.

Luis Cernuda (b. 1904) has been subject to several poetical isms, and is a poet of attractive intensity, delicate, suggestive, melodious. His *Perfil del aire* (*Profile of the Air*) was published in 1927, and his book of lyric prose, *Variaciones sobre un tema mexicano* in 1952. Cernuda has lived in exile since 1936.

In the same generation, many other poets have gained a considerable reputation. Among them may be mentioned: **Emilio Prados, Manuel Altolaguirre, Adriano del Valle, Juan Domenchina, Agustín de Foxá,** and **José María de Pemán.**

Still more noteworthy is **Rafael Alberti** (b. 1902). An ardent liberal and leftist always, he had the honor of defending Madrid in the Civil War and later of being expelled from the Communist party while he was in exile. His earlier volumes of verse, such as *Marinero en tierra* (1925) and succeeding volumes show his ability to absorb and express elements in the poetry of his native Andalusia. He has later been subject to various influences, notably surrealism, but he always puts his personal stamp, his true poetic facility in whatever he writes. His more recent work has shown greater spirituality. He selected what he considered most representative in his poetry in *Poesía* (1943).

The poet **Federico García Lorca** (1898-1936) was highly popular in his own country, and attracted more enthusiasm abroad than any Spanish poet of the century. His splendid career was cut off when, though he had no interest in politics, he was shot by Francoists in his native province of Granada at the outbreak of the Civil War.

Lorca published his first volume of verse, the *Libro de poemas,* in 1921, and *Canciones* in 1927. They give a foretaste of the appealing poetic qualities to be found in the *Romancero gitano* (*Gipsy Ballad Book,* 1928), widely received with enthusiastic acclaim. Lorca was in New York in 1930, though his surrealistic *Poeta en Nueva York* was not published until 1940. His *Poema del Cante Jondo* appeared after his return to Spain in 1931. The poignant *Llanto por Ignacio Sánchez Mejías* (translated as *Lament for the Death of a Bullfighter*) was published in 1935, his *Seis poemas gallegos* in 1936.

In only slightly lesser degree than Lope de Vega, Lorca succeeded in fusing deeply popular and highly sophisticated elements into a lovely poetic unity, which appeals to illiterates and to highly cultured audiences. Lorca's gift for melody is extraordinary and his poetic imagination startlingly vivid. He broods deeply over the eternal themes of love and death, with metaphors and symbols of unusual intensity and originality. Small wonder that his poems and plays have been so widely translated. Most Hispanists have had the joy of seeing eyes light up upon being asked: "Oh, do you know Lorca? I love him!"

Lorca's plays seemed to offer the best possibility of a renovation of the Spanish theater, but his style has not been followed. His *farsas,* such as *La zapatera prodigiosa* or *El amor de don Perlimplín con Belisa en su jardín* combine lightness, caricature, even the grotesque, with great poetic delicacy. Plays like *Mariana Pineda* and *Doña Rosita la soltera* tend to evoke a romantic past. Of deep intensity, with characters simplified though poetically symbolized, with most artistically used popular elements are *Bodas de sangre, Yerma, La casa de Bernarda Alba.*

LATER NOVELISTS

Members of the "Generation of 1898" such as Baroja, Benavente, and Juan Ramón Jiménez lived a long, long time, and continued to dominate the literary scene. Younger authors, however, with differing ideals, were making themselves heard, and some even like to speak of a "Generation of 1925." Those who began to write in the 'twenties were likely to be affected, either at home or later in exile, by the terrible Civil War of 1936-1939.

Arturo Barea (1897-1957), of humble origins, was heart and soul in favor of the Spanish Republic, which he served in various capacities until he was forced into exile in England. His chief novel, published first in English in three separate parts and then together as *The Forging of a Rebel,* in 1951. It is mainly autobiographical, and gives an admirable picture of a man who grew up in Spain just after the turn of the century, and no one who wishes to know the spiritual atmosphere of the times can afford to miss it. Barea also wrote a penetrating brief study of his fellow-countryman called *Lorca: the Poet and His People.*

Another convinced political liberal and ardent partisan of the Republic is **Ramón Sender** (b. 1902), widely translated abroad, and at present, presumably for political reasons, practically unmentioned in Spain. He has maintained his sturdy independence in exile in the United States, teaching (The

University of New Mexico) and writing assiduously. His first and quite popular novel was *Imán* (1929), a vivid account of his experiences as a soldier in Africa. Sender received the National Prize for Literature in Spain in 1935. He fought in the Spanish Civil War, as a Loyalist, of course, and his *Contraataque* (1937) is one of the best books to emerge from that dreadful conflict. *El lugar del hombre* (1940) is one of Sender's most neatly constructed works. *Crónica del alba* (1942) is an extremely delicate re-creation of the life and emotions of an eleven-year-old boy in Spain. Sender is still a vigorously productive author of novels on various themes and in various manners, dealing largely with man's place in society. In 1957 He published *Los cinco libros de Ariadna,* part of a quite vivid semi-autobiography. The author combines nineteenth-century naturalistic techniques with great imagination and deftness.

Probably most novel readers asked the question: "Who is the best novelist in Spain today?" would mention the name of **Camilo José Cela** (b. 1916), whose chief novels make grim reading. *La familia de Pascual Duarte* (1941) is supposedly the autobiography of a criminal awaiting execution, and characterized by stark realism and accounts of deeds of senseless violence. The novel is a fine example of a tendency labeled "Tremendismo," which has been followed by other authors. Cela's *La colmena* (*The Hive,* 1951) offers a most depressing picture of life in Madrid after the Civil War. The very numerous and unlovely characters, sharply etched by the author, are presented as victims of poverty and hunger. *La Catira* (*The Blonde,* 1955) has a Venezuelan setting. *El molino de viento* (*The Windmill*) appeared in 1956. Cela has also written poems, essays, short stories, and books of travel, and has been editing from his home in Mallorca a highly esteemed literary journal called *Los papeles de Son Armadans.*

Juan Antonio de Zunzunegui was born in 1901, in Bilbao, and the characters in his more than a dozen novels usually come from the financially secure classes in that city and in Madrid. Even though Zunzunegui was educated partly in England, France, and Italy, he remains strictly in the tradition of nineteenth-century Spanish realism, and his confessed model is Galdós. Critics have accused him of portraying life too much from the outside, too photographically. He began publishing regional sketches in 1926, and his first longer novel, *Chiripi* appeared in 1931. *El chiplichandle* (*The Ship Chandler*, 1939) presents types from the author's native Bilbao. *La quiebra* (*Bankruptcy*, 1947) enlarges on machinations in the business world. *El supremo bien* (1950) describes more idealistic characters. Other novels are *Esta obscura desbandada* (1952), *La vida como es* (1954), *El hijo hecho a contrata* (1956). Zunzunegui has been widely read in Spain though little abroad.

José María Gironella (b. 1917) is better known to foreigners. A frustrated seminary student, worker in a distillery, a grocery store, a clothing store, and a secondhand bookstore, and soldier for Franco during the Civil War, he won fame and the coveted Nadal Prize in 1946 with his first novel, *Un hombre* (translated into English as *The Soil Was Shallow*). *La marea* was published in 1948. His chief novel to date, winning critical attention at home and abroad and high praise from the author himself, is *Los cipreses creen en Dios* (1953). It is a long depiction of the spiritual atmosphere in Spain before the Civil War, and the scene is really the author's native Gerona. The narration of events tends to diminish the author's attention to his characters, and not all would agree that the picture is a fair one. The novel has run through many editions, and the author is a novelist of considerable talent, and perhaps greater achievements may be expected of him. The sequel to *Los cipreses* is *Un millón de muertos* (1961).

Of the numerous women novelists in Spain, the most popular has been **Carmen Laforet** (b. 1921). Her first novel, *Nada* (Nadal Prize, 1944) is vastly different in background and spirit from Cela's *Pascual Duarte,* and describes simply but vividly the life of a girl who comes to live in Barcelona. After devoting eight years solely to her husband and children, Carmen Laforet returned to literature with *La isla y los demonios* (the scene is the Canary Islands), in the same general style. *Una nueva mujer* (1955) is on the well-worn theme of the adulterous woman who repents and is regenerated by religion. Some critics esteem much more the novels of **Ana Maria Matute.**

Elena Quiroga (b. 1921) won the Premio Nadal in 1950 for her *Viento del norte,* and her *La sangre* (1952) won critical praise. Some have preferred her *Algo pasa en la calle* (1951).

Juan Goytisolo (b. 1931) is by many ranked next to Cela among living Spanish novelists. He represents a generation too young to participate in the Civil War and so having a different point of view. Goytisolo's *Duelo en el paraíso* (1955) skillfully tells the story of a group of children who had taken refuge during the war in a small Spanish village. *Juego de manos* really belongs to the preceding year. *La resaca* (*The Undertow*), the author's latest novel to date, was published in Paris and forbidden by the censorship in Spain. In English, *The Young Assassins* (1959) was well received. A younger brother, **Luis Goytisolo-Gay,** is also esteemed.

Luis Romero (b. 1916) received the Premio Nadal in 1951 for *La noria,* and is the author of various other novels. His technique is *tremendista,* and the complaint has been made that his numerous characters do not appear long enough for the reader to know them. Romero's attitude is in general pessimistic.

The list of others who have written novels recently in Spain, even of those who have received literary awards, would be long indeed. **Ignacio Agustí** won fame in 1943 with *Mariona Rebull.* **José Suárez Carreño,** also a dramatist and poet, won the Nadal Prize in 1949 with *Las últimas horas,* translated into English as *The Final Hours.* The journalist **Darío Fernández Flórez** shocked and lured the public with his crudely realistic *Lola, espejo oscuro.* **Enrique Azcoaga,** poet and art critic living in Buenos Aires, was considerably praised for his skillful portrayal of a type in *El empleado,* (1949) . **Tomás Salvador** (b. 1921) has written a dozen novels reflecting his experiences as a sort of government super-policeman. He considers *Cuerda de presos* (1953) his best.

The novel in Spain since 1936 has not yet equalled in excellence the production of the masters of the nineteenth century, but it shows promise.

DRAMATISTS AFTER BENAVENTE

Jacinto Benavente, during his long life, was the chief purveyor of plays to the Spanish stage and he lived until 1954.

Alejandro Casona (b. 1903) sprang into prominence during the Second Republic with *La sirena varada,* published in 1934. *Nuestra Natacha* was a great hit in Madrid in 1936.

Since 1937, Casona has lived in exile in Argentina, where he has enjoyed numerous successes: *La dama del alba* (1944), *La barca sin pescador* (1945), *Las árboles mueren de pie* (1949), *Siete gritos en el mar* (1951). Casona's plays are likely to be good theater, and to combine delicate fancy with realism.

Whatever may be the quality of the present day Spanish theater, there is at least no dearth of playwrights. In 1954, for example, there were 254 entries for the Premio Lope de Vega. Other prizes for plays are also offered. Foreign influences are in evidence—Ibsen, Pirandello, O'Neill, Sartre and others—and older dramatists such as Benavente are not forgotten.

Joaquín Calvo Sotelo (b. 1905) numbers theatrical successes among his numerous works, such as *Plaza de Oriente* and *La muralla* (1954), quite popular.

Enrique Jardiel Poncela (1901-1952) had numerous successes on the stage and possessed genuine humor, if not perfect dramatic effectiveness. One may mention *Usted tiene ojos de mujer fatal, Eloisa está debajo de un almendro, Los ladrones somos gente honrada.* The author died saddened because the public grew tired of his special manner.

Antonio Buero Vallejo (b. 1916) received the *Premio Lope de Vega* in 1949 for his *Historia de una escalera,* which with *costumbrista* elements, discloses episodes in the lives of various characters at various stages of their lives. Somewhat less popular success was enjoyed by *En la ardiente oscuridad* (1950). *La tejedora de sueños* (1952) is based on Homer's *Odyssey. La madrugada* (1953) increased the author's reputation. *Hoy es fiesta* (1956) combines symbolism with realism. *Las cartas boca abajo* (1957) is a psychological play. Buero Vallejo's most recent drama to date is *Un soñador para un pueblo,* historical in nature. Buero Vallejo seems to represent a positive value in the mid-twentieth century Spanish theater.

José López Rubio (b. 1903) combines a good sense of humor and phantasy with sound theatrical construction. In 1928 he and **Eduardo Ugarte** wrote the quite successful *De la noche a la mañana,* and in 1930 *La casa de naipes.* After a period of work for the movies, he returned to the stage in 1949 with *Alberto. Celos del aire* (1950) is by some regarded as his most finished play. *La otra orilla* presents a fanciful confrontation of attitudes between the living and the dead. López Rubio won the Premio Nacional de Teatro in 1954 for his *La venda en los ojos.*

Other playwrights have endeavored to rehabilitate the Spanish stage. The fluent conservative propagandist and author of all sorts of works **José María Pemán** (b. 1898) has written numerous plays, of which the best is perhaps *Edipo* (1954). Other dramatists worthy of mention are **Miguel Mihura,** who has a gay sense of unsubtle humor, **Víctor Ruiz Iriarte, Alfonso Paso, Soriano de Andía,** and **J. A. Giménez Arnau.** Some consider the most promising of the younger dramatists to be **Alfonso Sastre** (b. 1926). Even if his inspiration is often bookish, his technique is good, especially in dialogue. Among his works may be mentioned *Escuadra hacia la muerte, La mordaza, La sangre de Dios,* and *Muerte en el barrio.* Audiences do not know or care if the report is true that he writes with green and red ink.

CONTEMPORARY THINKERS, ESSAYISTS, AND SCHOLARS

Quite apart from religious or political propagandists, serious thinkers and scholars have done their work in Spain, or outside of it, during and since the Civil War. **Pedro Laín Entralgo** (b. 1908), studied medicine in Madrid and psychiatry in Vienna. He was professor and then rector of the University of Madrid until he was deposed for political reasons. He has been one of several Spanish doctors who turned from medicine toward more general problems of culture. He has a keen sense of traditional Spanish values and very wide cosmopolitan outlook. In addition to various books on medicine, he has written a study of Menéndez y Pelayo, *Las generaciones en la historia* (1945), *La generación del noventa y ocho* (1945; one of the best meditations on that generation), and *España como problema* (1949), plus numerous essays and discourses. He has had considerable influence on younger writers and thinkers, and one looks forward with interest to his work in the future.

The able critic **Guillermo de Torre** (b. 1900) vigorously supported such advanced literary movements as vanguardism, and he was often regarded as the apostle and prophet of all that was most modern. He has published valuable studies of Picasso and Apollinaire. He edited various magazines, wrote poems, translated from the French, and edited several authors foreign and native, including the poems of his friend García Lorca.

José Luis Aranguren (b. 1909), Professor of Ethics in the University of Madrid, is one of the Spaniards who is most familiar with advanced Catholic thought in Europe. One of his better-known works is *Catolicismo y protestantismo como formas de existencia* (1952).

Julián Marías (b. 1914), pupil of Ortega y Gasset, has been a prolific writer on philosophical and literary themes. He has produced stimulating studies of Ortega and Unamuno, and general works on past and contemporary philosophy. His literary criticism is acute. He has lectured extensively in the United States.

José Ferrater Mora (b. 1909), a Catalan who has lived in exile since 1939 and whose thought is by no means considered to be within the bounds of Catholic orthodoxy, has produced several volumes of philosophical studies. Among his works may be mentioned the particularly able *Diccionario de la filosofía* (1941), *Unamuno* (1944), *Cuestiones españolas* (1946), *Ortega y Gasset* (1957).

Ricardo Gullón (b. 1908) is a broadly trained, knowledgeous and acute critic.

Attention has already been invited to the very large number of thinkers, critics, and scholars now existing in Spain and abroad.

POETS. THE THIRTIES UNTIL NOW

In the nineteen-thirties, poets who had established them-selves early in the century, such as Juan Ramón Jiménez and the Machados, were continuing their work, while poets representing various newer isms were continuing theirs. The tendency of younger poets who came into prominence in the nineteen-thirties seemed to represent an effort to return to simpler and more classic forms, compose less dehumanized verse, with greater attention to the theme of love.

Three poets were especially significant, Rosales, Panero and Vivanco. **Luis Rosales** (b. 1910) in his volume *Abril* (1935), showed classic influences, particularly that of Garcilaso. His poems, including those in his collection *Rimas* (1951) are often religious, generally personal.

Leopoldo Panero (b. 1909) may be best represented by *Canto personal* (1953), all written in tercets. His poems touch everyday experiences and emotions, expressed in an uncomplicated manner. His brother **Juan Panero** (1908-1937) wrote usually in long meters, and is noted for delicacy as well as depth.

Luis Felipe Vivanco (b. 1907), an architect by profession, has translated Paul Claudel and Rainer Maria Rilke. As shown by his earlier poems and by *Continuación de la vida* (1948), his note is mainly religious, and his expression clear and simple. He has been called a more melodious Unamuno in poetry.

Miguel Hernández (1910-1942), farm laborer and goat-herd, became familiar with poetic forms from Garcilaso through Góngora, but put his personal and original stamp on his own poems. His premature death cut short one of the most promising careers of his day, but he has exerted considerable influence. His most important collection of verse may be found in *Perito en lunas*.

Dionisio Ridruejo (b. 1912), a restless and controversial political figure has mainly adhered to poems classic in form but approaching every subject human and divine. In collaboration with **Pedro Laín Entralgo,** he founded the influential literary review *Escorial*. Ridruejo's verse may be esteemed by reading his own anthology, *En once años* (1950).

The number of practicing poets in Spain is long, and

choice among them is arbitrary. The following names may be suggested: **Victoriano Crémer** (b. 1910), **Gabriel Celaya** (b. 1911), **José Luis Cano** (b. 1912), **José García Nieto** (b. 1914), **Germán Bleiberg** (b. 1915), **José Luis Hidalgo** (1919-1947), **Vicente Gaos** (b. 1919), **Rafael Morales** (b. 1919), **Carlos Bousoño** (b. 1923. His reputation is growing.), **José María Valverde** (b. 1923), **Concha Zardoya, José Hierro, Blas de Otero, Eugenio de Nora, Angela Figueroa, Gloria Fuertes, Ramon de Garciasol, Carmen Conde, Jaime Ferrán.** Many other poets, some very young, might be added to the list. One observes in reading many of these poets a spirit of protest, a great social and moral conciousness, an abandonment of ornamentation, a refusal to write verse that is merely pretty and musical.

The lyric voice has never been silenced in Spain, and will not be.

A Few Useful References

History of Spain

Altamira, R., *A History of Spain*. New York, 1949. The best
    one-vol. history.
Livermore, H., *A History of Spain*. London, 1958. No tables
    or lists. History brought barely up to 1950.
Madariaga, S. de, *Spain*. New York, 1958. Fine background book.
Castro, Américo, *The Structure of Spanish History*, Princeton,
    1954. Highly stimulating meditations.
Diccionario de historia de España. 2 vols., Madrid, 1952. Nearly
    3,000 pages of useful information.

Recent History

Rodríguez-Castellano, J., *Introducción a la historia de España*. New
    York, 1956. Good, short textbook. Illustrated.
Brenan, Gerald, *The Spanish Labyrinth*. New York, 1943.
Pritchett, V. S., *The Spanish Temper*. New York, 1954.
Matthews, Herbert, *The Yoke and the Arrows*. New York, 1957.
    Careful dissection of the Franco régime by a thoroughly capa-
    ble journalist. Highly recommended.
Likely to be controversial. 2d. ed. New York, 1961.

Books of Travel

Brenan, Gerald, *The Face of Spain*. New York, 1956. Good.
Crockett, Lucy H., *Kings Without Castles*. New York, 1957. Honest
    impressions of a 10,000 mile trip by automobile through Spain
    by a shrewd observer.
Since the seventeenth century, at least hundreds of authors have
published their impressions, and the process continues. Numerous
novels, Spanish and foreign, have their background in Spain and
are most informative.

Spanish Civilization

Peers, E. A., *Spain, a Companion to Spanish Studies*. 5th ed., re-
    vised and enlarged by R. F. Brown, London, 1956. Useful,
    though not brought up to date.

Mallo, J., *España. Síntesis de su civilización.* New York, 1957. Good class textbook. Illustrated.

Adams, N. B., *The Heritage of Spain.* Revised ed., New York, 1959. Brief treatment of Spanish history and culture, especially literature. Illustrated. Bibliographies.

Histories of Spanish Literature

Northup, G. T., *An Introduction to Spanish Literature.* Chicago 1925, 1936. A standard book, straightforward, useful. An ed. revised by N. B. Adams was published in 1960.

Del Río, A., *Historia de la literatura española.* 2 vols., New York, 1948. Excellent presentation of facts and criticism.

Hurtado, J. and González-Palencia, A., *Historia de la literatura española.* 6th ed., Madrid, 1949. 1049 pages. Extremely useful for facts and bibliography.

Valbuena Prat, A., *Historia de la literatura española.* 5th ed., 3 vols., Barcelona, 1957. Uneven but very suggestive.

Brenan, G., *The Literature of the Spanish People.* Meridian Books, 1957. Despite defects, most attractively written. Recommended.

Chandler, Kessel and Schwartz, Kessel, *A New History of Spanish Literature.* Baton Rouge, 1961. Large, thorough. Recommended.

Bibliography

Simón Díaz, J., *Bibliografía de la literatura hispánica,* 4 vols. to date, Madrid, 1950–1956.

Serís, H., *Bibliografía de la literatura española.* 2 vols. to date. Syracuse, 1948–1954.

Bleiberg, G. and Julián Marías, *Diccionario de la literatura española.* 2d. ed., Madrid, 1953. Inclusive to date, and invaluable for quick reference.

Newmark, M., *Dictionary of Spanish Literature.* New York, 1956. Defective but useful.

Collections of Texts

Biblioteca de Autores Españoles. 71 vols., Madrid, 1846–1880. New vols. now being added. Vast compilation, useful when better texts are not available.

Clásicos Castellanos. About 150 vols. to date, in general well edited.

There are many other collections of Spanish texts, in the past, or still being published. The fine leather-bound volumes from M. Aguilar and other publishers and the recommendable paperbacks of the *Colección Austral* and others are steadily making Spanish literature more accessible.

Anthologies

Del Río, A., *Antología general de la literatura española*. 2 vols., New York, 1954. 2d. ed. 1960. Large and useful

There are a great many anthologies of Spanish literature, especially of poetry. One might begin with *The Oxford Book of Spanish Verse*, 2d. ed. Oxford, 1940 and *The Penguin Book of Spanish Verse*, Penguin Books, 1956.

The Spanish Language

Entwistle, Wm. J., *The Spanish Language*. Oxford, 1936.

Spaulding, R. K., *How Spanish Grew*. Berkeley, 1953.

Lapesa, R., *Historia de la lengua española*. 4th ed., Madrid, 1957.

Dictionaries of Spanish

Unfortunately Webster's *Unabridged* and the *New English Dictionary* have no counterparts in Spanish.

For those of English speech, very useful dictionaries are:

Williams, E. B., *Holt Spanish Dictionary*, New York, 1955; *Appleton's Revised Cuyás Spanish Dictionary*, 4th ed., New York, no date; *Cassell's Spanish Dictionary*, London 1959, and New York, 1960: the most recent in the field.

For Spanish grammar, a very useful volume is:

Ramsay, M. M., *A Textbook of Modern Spanish*. Rev. by R. K. Spaulding. New York, 1956.

Journals

Information and criticism concerning Spanish literature will be found in the following periodical publications. Many offer book reviews and bibliography. This list is quite selective among journals now being published: *Revista de filología española, Nueva revista de filología hispánica. Hispanic Review, Hispania, Bulletin hispanique, Bulletin of Hispanic Studies, Revista de literatura, The Modern Language Journal, Hispanic American Report* (contemporary history), *Indice, Insula,* Hispanófila, Modern Language Notes, *Romance Notes, Revista Hispánica Moderna, Cuadernos, Cuadernos Hispanoamericanos.* Many other journals publish at least occasional articles of interest to Hispanophiles.

INDEX